Happily Ever-After

By

Sandra LaFaye Crump

This book is a work of fiction. Places, events, and situations in this story are purely fictional. Any resemblance to actual persons, living or dead, is coincidental.

ISBN: 1-4033-6728-0 (e-book)
ISBN: 1-4033-6729-9 (Paperback)

This book is printed on acid free paper.

1stBooks - rev. 07/02/03

DEDICATIONS AND THANK YOU'S

First of all, I dedicate this book to my Savior and Lord, Jesus Christ. He blesses the work of my hands; He gives me wisdom and favor in all that I do. My honors and rewards are all dedicated back to him. He is the one who Promotes and Exalts. God is working on me and within me, more and more. I praise and magnify His name.

This book is a testimony of my suffering but also, it is the story of how God has brought me from darkness into light and how he's turned my mourning into a dance of joy.

Next, this story is dedicated to my parents: Pastor Earl and Earnestine Crump, the best parents in the world. They never tried making decisions for me; they gave me Godly counsel and told me that it was up to me to make the proper choice. They encouraged me to walk the proper path and to live a holy life. From childhood, I've been taught the Bible, how to live with God and how to hide God's word in my heart.

God blesses me because of my parent's obedience to God. Thank you, Mom and Dad, for being there for me. For cheering me on in victory, comforting me in times of trouble, and loving me through it all. I thank God every day for you both and you as my role model in ministry, in marriage and in family. I'll love you both forever. When I grow up, I want to be like you both.

Next I dedicate this to my brothers, Earl and Joshua. You two are truly brothers. You have gotten on my nerves most of the days of my life but I can see how you allowed God to use you to make me stronger. When I returned back home after my divorce, you didn't criticize me or mock me or my situation; instead, you gave me encouraging words like, "You deserve better," etc. I love you for that. You've given me reasons to laugh and it felt so good to be around someone who loved me and who always made me laugh.

To my sister and brother-in-law, Cassandra and Reginald Hayes - you two are an inspiration to me, to see you both happy and living in prosperity. Your encouraging words and fellowship have kept me going and I love you so much for this. I could always call upon you both and during my hard times, I could cry on your shoulder. You allowed me to go to your house and stay for hours and, without saying one word, you knew the pain that I was experiencing. Thank you, forever. I owe you, big time. I love being around you.

To my beautiful niece, Ms. Breya Hayes - you may never know how much I really needed to hold you and for you to be around me. That first day that I came back to live with my parents, I really didn't want to be around anyone. I cried and cried and your mother,

Cassandra, said encouraging words to me, "Here's Breya, talk to Faye Faye."

Breya, I know that at the time, you couldn't talk. You were only four months old. Just holding you in my arms and seeing your smile gave me so much pleasure. You'll never know! It was like you could feel how I was hurting and I know if you could have talked, you would really have encouraged me. People wonder why I treat you like my own daughter. I would give you my whole pay check and wouldn't think a thing about it. At my job, I have almost all of your pictures surrounding my cube. Breya, you are really an inspiration to me and I will always love you. Hey, if you ever need anything, you can always ask me, Tee Tee Faye.

To my oldest sister, Roschunda Williams; I've spent so much time flying to and fro, from Detroit to St. Louis. I really appreciate all of your words, our talks and the laughter that have helped me through the difficult times. I still have a lot of things to laugh about; you are really cool to be around. I love you.

To my friend, Essie Simpson, who was there and who knew what I've been going through. Although there were things that I couldn't tell you, I knew that you were praying for me.

Thanks to Rosemary Smith, Felicia Davis, Natasha Gamble, Kimberly Simmons, Sharon Askins, Robin Moraskey, Sandy Valken, Stephanie Jackson, Angela

Barham, Veronica Seatts, Yvette Searcy, Ernine Porter, Shawn Bracewell, Sandra Washington, Rev. Nelson, Shaquana Burton, Germaine Love: I really appreciate all of the emails and encouraging words, and your support. I'll never forget the kindness that you've shown me. Thanks.

To Michelle Barham: Cousin, I love ya! Thanks for going to Cancun, Mexico, with me and helping me to relax and forget about my cares in the *Estados Unidos* (smile). You have been a prayer partner and a best friend. You will never know how much I appreciate you for being yourself. Thanks for receiving my phone calls which, most of the time, were cries for help. Even though you may not answer the phone at 3 a.m., I appreciate that you returned my calls and had lunches with me and encouraged me in the Lord. I'm glad that you're here in the States; the phone calls will be cheaper. Thanks for being my Elizabeth. Whenever I have a dream or a vision about where I would like to be in my life, you see the same thing that I do and, also, that we're on the same level.

Diva-licious. Hey Michelle, never forget, "Hey, Margarita." (smile)

To my grandparents; to the Dixon's and Crump's; to my aunt's, uncle's and sister's in Christ; to my cousins, co-workers, group leaders, managers, my ex-mother-in-law, etc., do not want to name names 'cause I don't want to leave anyone out but you all were always there for me, to build me up. You kept me in your prayers and I love you; may God forget not your labor of love.

To my friend, Jimmy Bryant: You are indeed a sweet person. Thank you for encouraging me and being a friend when I needed one. Thanks for singing me a song.

To my friend, Aaron Shaw: Thank you for all of your encouraging words. Thank you for making me laugh and for giving me hypothetical analysis of everything, and thank you for making me smile. You are, indeed, a good friend.

To my friend, Dorinda Gibbs: I wouldn't hear the end of it if I did not give a shout out to a sweet person whom I've known for such a time; we have shared some deep issues. You're the best; I'm glad that you're looking up to me, as I look to Jesus and hopefully, I'll make a difference in your life. Take care, and stay in school.

To my friend and coworker, Carlos Colon: You really know when to lay on the compliments! Your sweet words have gained you a friend. Thanks for being there when I needed someone to talk.

To Mr. Melody: Now what would singing be, if I'd never heard you sing to me. Oh, that rhymes. I am glad that I have gotten to know the real you. You're a good person and you've shared a great deal of "what men think," and I'm glad that I got the chance to hear it from you. When you make it big time, forget not the Smiling Woman 27.

To Joshua Jewett: What all can I say about you? You're my best friend, big brother, confidante, one who listens and sometimes laughs with me and at me. You're an all-around friend and I'm glad that we've gotten the chance to become close. I mean, who would have thought that I would need someone from Ohio to keep me on track. You'll never be forgotten and no matter where we both are in our lives or in the world, we'll always remain best friends. I love you, brother (you and me shall never part...from the Color Purple Movie - smile.)

To Larry Warner: What a manager! Who knew that a manager could be a listening ear, a man of authority and a father-figure, and all at work? Wow! Now I know why you're called The Hammer. Ha Ha. Thanks for encouraging me and sitting down with me, as if I were your daughter. Thanks for being there for me at work.

Finally, I can't forget my church. I love you, my church family. Thank you for the prayers, love and support and the encouragement to go on in everything. Just as *Luke 6:40*, *"When a disciple is fully trained, he shall be like his teacher." (NIV)*

Just knowing that if there were no one else to believe in me, my church family has "got my back", along with *GOODNESS AND MERCY*, who's *following me all the days of my life*.

Pastor says that we're going to another level, that we may expect turnaround and that is in full effect, and I say that it is so in your lives, as well. I love you.

To Janice Elkins: Thank you so much for giving me professional assistance on my manuscript. You are truly a blessing from God.

Table of Contents

INTRODUCTION

This book is all about me, Sandra L. Crump. Many people think they know me as a person. Some do; others, however, may find this story a revelation. My life as a young adult started off OK and then became awesome. Later, I faced a great terror and depression that, in the end, in spite of the many troubled times I went through, resulted in a satisfying victory.

The information in this book is meant to help people who feel that they have to keep everything inside. It is to try to teach my friends and readers that it is all right to talk to someone, to get Godly counsel. One thing I've learned as a young adult is that no matter who makes mistakes, great or small, God is always there with an escape plan and because He always works things out for our spiritual benefit, we are able to live with His choice.

After reading this story, some people may think that the beginning of my adult life was rough but in the end, I was closer to God and to the Word of God. This usually happens when we go through tests and trials - we draw closer to God.

It is very hard to be a Pastor's Kid (P.K.). People tend to place you on a mountain top and assume that you will never make a mistake because if you did, it would reflect upon your parents and the ministry. Needless to say, I didn't like this assumption. People should realize that children who grow up in a minister's family are human, too. Most of the time if mistakes are made, they aren't intentional. God is merciful and forgives us and he cleanses us from unrighteousness, *for whom the Son sets free is free, indeed.* So if God can forgive others, we should be able to forgive, also, and I'd like to say to those who thought they understood my martial bliss but saw fit to discuss my personal issues and business in the streets, I forgive you and I love you.

This isn't a fairy tale or a fictitious story. The characters are fictitious but the moral and actual contents are true and deal with the highs and lows of my marital bliss.

This narrative not only explains what I've gone through but also what I'm presently achieving. There are those who think they know me and some people may think that emulating me is worthwhile, not realizing that we all go through different stages in life. Each of us needs to achieve our own ultimate goal - conquering our personal mountain while reaching for loftier heights and deeper depths.

I want you to read this story as if you were walking in my shoes, to feel the pain I felt and to experience my relationship with the men in my life. There are many choices that we make that determines how things eventually work out. You are the only person who can make your decisions. Even in the Bible, God allowed Adam and Eve to decide which Tree they would choose. He could have told them to eat from the Tree of Life but that would have meant He would violate their will, so God gave them options. It was up to them to make their own decision so in the end, if something went wrong, they could not blame God for their mistake.

This book and its contents aren't written to put down or to belittle my ex-husband. I wish only good things for him in the future. I just want him to know that I have forgiven him and do not hold anything against him and to let him know that God has forgiven him. In the beginning. we had a brother and sister relationship and this grew into friendship. It didn't last; its outcome wasn't favorable but our friendship has lasted. Perhaps our relationship didn't have the right purpose or perhaps we married the wrong person. One thing I have to say to my former husband: "It's because of you that I ran to the Throne of Grace and obtained God's mercy in my time of need. I got closer to the Lord and I am now enjoying His benefits."

God has so much for us but until we get connected to the spout where the glory comes out, we remain immature and inefficient. God has something for you and someone for you; however, in order to receive it all, *Seek ye first the kingdom and his righteousness and all these things* [that you desire] *shall be added to you (Matthew 6:33 KJV).*

Our marriage wasn't unhappy all the time. Since it ended in divorce, the Devil meant our union to harm us but God turned it around and it resulted in positive things for us. God is the only one who knows what tomorrow will bring.

If you abide in me and my words abide in you, you can ask what you will and it shall be done unto you {John 15:7 KJV). And finally, *God is able to do exceeding, abundantly, above all that you can ask or think, according to the power that worketh in you (Ephesians 3:20 KJV).*

God will keep you in perfect peace, whose mind is stayed on him. In his presence is fullest of joy. The Lord God is a sun and shield; the Lord giveth grace and glory; no good thing will he withhold from them that walk up rightly (Psalms 84:11 KJV).

One thing have I desired of the Lord that will I seek after, that I may dwell in the house of the Lord all the days of my life, to behold the beauty of the Lord and to inquire in his temple. For in the time of trouble, he shall hide me in his pavilion; he shall hide me in the secret of his tabernacle (Psalms 27:4- KJV).

If you obey and serve me, you shall spend your days in prosperity and your years in Pleasures (Job 36:11 KJV)

NOTES FOR THE READER

CHAPTER ONE

EARLY DAYS OF YOUNG ADULTHOOD

There is a lady whose name is Tresa and her age is 24. She grew up in a house where the word of God was taught to her and to her brothers and sisters. It was a tradition to learn God's word and to pray to him for everything. All through life, the rules at home, based on the Bible, were strictly obeyed. Tresa's father was a minister and God saw fit to ordain him, to make him a Pastor and the leader of his people. This meant strict enforcement of the truths in the Bible; unholy living wasn't an option.

Some of the things that people Tresa's age had an opportunity to do, and places that other's were able to go were totally out of the question for her. She eventually adjusted to these limitations. Although she didn't think that her lifestyle was unfair, some of her friends did but she let them know up front that her Christian way of life was not just to please her parents or because of her upbringing, it was her personal choice - she enjoyed focusing upon pleasing God.

After she graduated from high school, Tresa needed to establish herself, to achieve something that would prove she was really special. She enrolled as a student at Ross Medical Educational Center but she had poor study habits. She prayed to God for guidance and immediately the subjects became easier for her to understand. After she completed the course and received her grades, she found that she had made all A's. She cried with joy and excitedly praised God, knowing that he is the One who deserves all of the credit.

NOTES FOR THE READER

CHAPTER TWO

FINDING EMPTINESS INSIDE

Tresa wanted to obtain a college degree; she began by taking a business course at the local community college. She was excited when she received a B in her first course. She enrolled in another business course and again, she did extremely well. The following winter she decided to take a break from college. She worked as a medical biller in a laboratory; she enjoyed this job very much. Her colleagues shared information with her and she was able to apply this knowledge to her work projects and this, in turn, enabled her to improve her work habits and techniques.

She attended church regularly and enjoyed the bible studies that her father taught. Still, she felt a void in her life. Well, you've guessed it! She realized she needed a male companion. Over the years, she had come into contact with men and when she had begun a friendship, in the end it had always turned sour. Many tears and much pain had come from past relationships. She had met some really strange men who had strange ways; one was part of the new age movement. Until he explained, she couldn't perceive what this meant. He told her that he was her savior and that they were individually superior, and all of that weird jazz. She

4

knew almost immediately that they had nothing in common because when she invited him to go to church with her he would invite her to go on a picnic, instead, and he would include his daughter.

Tresa next came into contact with a very immature man. His life revolved around his friends so she knew he wasn't the one, either. With the next guy, however, it was like love at first sight. This man bought her whatever her heart desired. She once mentioned a diamond tennis bracelet and the following day during lunch, she owned one. He would bring her ultimate all-time favorite lunch, Taco Bell, to her office. He also gave her gifts such as teddy bears, clothing, roses, cards, candy - whatever was available, he would buy for her. Every morning she went to work with a smile on her face. Her co-workers knew that her boy friend gave her something new every day because she placed the floral arrangements, bears, candy, balloons, love letters and other gifts in her cubicle. She knew that her co-workers were jealous. Her parents and sister were shocked; they realized there was something wrong with this picture. Tresa gave him nothing and he gave her the world.

In December, he asked her what she wanted out of a serious relationship. Next thing she knew, he had told her that he wanted to marry her. They decided the ceremony would be the following November. Tresa's head was way up in the clouds and her face glowed with pleasure. After their relationship became serious, the friend from work who had introduced them sat with her in church.

Tresa asked her fiance to come to the New Year's Eve church service and he accepted. She wore an Elvira black evening gown and she was a knockout. When they arrived, Tresa took his arm and as they entered the church, all eyes were upon them. When the usher escorted them down the isle, people were whispering because they looked so good together. They sat close to the front. Church had never been this exciting; Tresa had a man! This was so awesome!

After the service was over, her friend wanted to talk to Tresa's father so they entered the Pastor's office. Tresa wondered what was going on but she decided that her friend just wanted to meet her father. Finally, her father asked her to step outside and she did but she tried to overhear their conversation. Her boyfriend was asking her father if he could court his daughter! Tresa thought that was so romantic. She was really in love.

After they left the church, Tresa and her friend went into the fellowship hall and ate breakfast; later, everyone went home. Tresa's parents wanted to know all about her friend. They asked her who this person was and what church he attended and where he was employed. Tresa's friend attended a church where her parents had recently been members, so Tresa's father had him investigated. He soon came back to Tresa with information that her friend wanted to marry her, but that he had been married previously and had never divorced. Her father also informed her about some very serious charges against her boyfriend. Tresa's heart fell. She never dreamed that someone who had given her everything could be so wrong for her. She continued to go out on dates with him, but she also went on with her life.

Tresa began to have the feeling that she was being watched and followed. She would see the familiar face of one of her father's parishioner's and she also began to see him at her job, as well as other people whom she had not seen before. One day as she was leaving home, she could have sworn that she was being followed. This frightened her so much that she became a little paranoid.

One Sunday after church, Tresa's friends wanted to go bowling. Her boyfriend was there and everyone was having a good time. All of a sudden she heard a voice from four lanes over, "I know she's not with him. He's a married man. He's married to this lady at my church." What a great drama! The girl who had spoken was a member of Tresa's church and, one by one, people started to leave. Tresa's friend began acting like a fool.

"I don't know that woman so why should we leave?" he asked.

"Well, I do," Tresa responded, "and she knows my father and I think that we should leave before she tells him."

The person who had been driving Tresa around was with them, so she took Tresa to a restaurant because her boyfriend wasn't ready to go home. After they arrived at the restaurant they found everyone was tripping out, saying they couldn't believe that Tresa's boyfriend was still married, which embarrassed her. After dinner, when Tresa went home she learned that father had already been informed about her actions by the loud-mouthed lady from the bowling alley. He confronted his daughter, commanding her to leave that man alone. She went to her room and cried. When this friend called her, she told him that she wasn't allowed to be around him anymore. This upset him and he said some mean things about Tresa's father and about his own pastor.

Tresa thought then that her life was over. She was afraid to go to church, not knowing how much the congregation knew about the incident at the bowling alley the previous Sunday. She did go but she arrived late and left early, trying to dodge everyone and all their comments.

There were days when members of her friend's church attended her church. When this happened, it made Tresa nervous. She arrived at the church and went in but before she could get to her chair, the loud-mouthed lady made a smart remark and Tresa went home in tears. This went on for more than a year. Finally, Tresa realized she couldn't live like that any longer. She went up for an altar call and asked God to help her get over the, another one began. Tresa was sitting in church, minding her own business, when this guy started starring and smiling at her. How confusing! What was his problem?

After church, Tresa was approached by a girl who said there was going to be a cookout at her house and she asked Tresa to stop by. Since Tresa had never been to this girl's house, she realized that something new was about to happen to her so she responded to the invitation. When the girl met Tresa at the door, she was smiling from ear to ear. She asked Tresa to sit down and then she offered to prepare a plate of food for her. Tresa was wondering what was up when a guy came out of nowhere and began trying to talk to her. Tresa didn't really know what to think of him. She had just finished an involvement with a man who had lied to her and she wasn't sure she wanted to enter into another.

At first, Tresa's relationship with her new friend was OK. He was a Romeo. He would arrive at her job even before she did, with breakfast for her and a juice. He would bring roses, flowers, bears, etc. This was very familiar, and she was very cautious. Still, she thought that it was possible that he could be the one, but she wanted to start out slow and take her time.

After two weeks, this man asked Tresa to go to a certain park. She accepted his invitation and after they arrived, he gave her an engagement ring. Tresa almost fainted. She was thinking, 'How can he give me an engagement ring when we haven't even been dating?" She decided to accept the ring but later, she thought really hard about it and returned it as well as the other gifts that he had given to her.

During this time, Tresa was working a second job at a department store. She would receive phone calls from her new friend while she was at work. Many nights after her second job ended and she left work, when she got to her car she noticed that the cards that she had given to this man were on her windshield. This was very scary. It felt like a fatal attraction or something; it was a nightmare. Finally, one day this guy came to the store where Tresa was working the register and he screamed out her name and that he loved her. Everyone applauded but Tresa wanted to hide under a rock, she was so frustrated. At church she sat alone and this man would come in and sit beside her and smile. Tresa didn't want to sit near him, so she would get up and move so she could sit next to her mom, but he also moved. He called her mom Mother. Tresa hated this. He purchased gifts for her mother and her brother; it seemed to her that he did this just to upset her.

One day during church there was an altar call for those in the congregation who were depressed. Tresa went up to the altar and the anointing was so strong, it started to break the yokes and bondages that had bound her. When she came back to herself, she noticed that this guy standing behind her was saying, "In the name of Jesus, devil lose her from the strong holds, etc."

This was comical because he was the reason Tresa was depressed in the first place, and he had the nerve to pray over her!

NOTES FOR THE READER

CHAPTER 3

A CHANGE OF PLANS

One day Tresa met a man at her church whom she really enjoyed being around. She attended many single functions that he also attended and they soon became friends. Eventually their relationship became more than just friendship. Tresa thought about him often. He invited her over to his house for dinner and to watch videos, and they also went bowling and to the movies. When she didn't see him regularly, she thought her heart would break.

There were many disagreements between them but Tresa always thought positive thoughts and she felt that things would change. This guy's name was Paul. Tresa realized that at times she got on his nerves but there were times that she thought Paul was just being mean. Still, Tresa felt in her heart that this man really loved her. He often asked others what kind of person Tresa was and when she was around him, she was sure of the way he felt about her.

In her mind they were dating although Paul said it was only a friendship. They frequently double-dated with other couples. Everyone around them seemed to know that they were meant for each other. By the time

13

they had known each other for a year, Tresa couldn't wait to talk to Paul to see how his days and nights were going, so she called him daily. He would respond to her questions with harsh remarks such as, "Stop calling me!" and "Stop paging me," or, "I get all of your messages," or, "I'll call you when I have something to talk about."

When this happened, after Tresa hung up the phone she would cry. She couldn't understand why Paul was so mean to her when he couldn't wait to have her over to his house, or to hang out with her. One day he would call her and they would talk for hours and his conversation would be so deep that Tresa would laugh and cry, but on other days he would cut Tresa off and say that he was about to go out, or that he was busy with company. At these times he responded to her in a mean way. Also, there were days when Paul told Tresa not to talk with his mom all the time. Tresa thought that perhaps Paul was jealous because his mother spent time with her and not with him.

Tresa and Paul's mom and his aunt went to Sea World for a weekend. It was so much fun. Paul's mom and aunt were great to be around. They felt like sister's on a girl's vacation; they talked and laughed for hours. Later, Tresa and her family, along with her friend Stephanie, went to Disney World and then on a cruise. Paul picked up Tresa and her friend and drove them to the airport, and he hung out with them until their plane took off. Tresa's father remarked that he thought Paul couldn't wait until Tresa got back.

The week passed quickly and when Tresa and Stephanie returned, Paul picked them up at the airport. Later, Paul took Tresa to church. When they went in and sat down together, she had a big smile on her face. Members of the congregation told her that Paul hadn't attended church during the time she had been in Florida. The following year Paul's mom, his aunt and Tresa went to Jamaica for a week. What an exciting trip! It was a joy, hanging out with them. After the week ended and they returned, Paul was at the airport to pick them up and it was obvious that he had missed her.

Their friendship progressed and Tresa wanted Paul to attend her father's 50th birthday celebration. He didn't purchase a ticket so Tresa bought one for him and he did attend, and he enjoyed himself. The following day, Paul went to Tresa's father and asked him for her hand in marriage. When Tresa found this out she was shocked because Paul had never encouraged anything other than a brother and sister relationship. She became excited because she was really in love with Paul, although she knew by his actions that he loved her with reservations. It was like he loved her but he was only going to display a little affection, like he couldn't give her all of himself, only the part that he wanted to share with her.

One day Paul asked Tresa to go out for dinner and she agreed. They met after work and went to the Red Lobster, but the waitress took so long to seat them that

Tresa suggested they go to a Mexican place that she loved. They did, and she ordered the usual virgin lime margarita and chips and cheese/salsa dip. While they were talking and laughing, Paul reached under the table and pulled out the largest and most beautiful, extravagant wedding ring that Tresa could have imagined, a large Marquette cut diamond with baguettes on each side. She knew this ring must have cost Paul a fortune; it had probably set him back a few months on his bills. When Paul proposed, she was speechless.

The waitress served their appetizers and this destroyed the romantic moment. Still, Tresa was delighted and she could hardly wait to get home to show her parents and her sister; she was wearing the biggest smile in the world. She felt like a queen who had been given the royal treatment.

When she arrived home she immediately went to show her father, who was in the garage. She didn't say much, just waved her hand in the air in front of him. He smiled, and the smile was the one he used when one of his children graduated from college. He was very happy for Tresa. He told her to go to her mom's place of employment and show her mother the ring. Tresa realized that this event was to change her life. She went to her mother's job and knocked on the door. Her smile lit up the hallway and as she entered, her mother wondered why Tresa's face had such a glow! Tresa flashed the ring and a little tear escaped down her mother's cheek, She told Tresa that she was very proud of her. This was the nicest feeling that Tresa had had in a long time. It was like, "Now it's my turn to be honored," and she knew that God had not forgotten her.

Later, the news reached the rest of Tresa's family as well as the people at her job and her church. There were people who came from all over to look at the ring, which became known as the 'ring of the year'. Tresa was the talk of the town.

Wedding preparations were put into motion, many plans began to form and decisions were made. More and more people wanted to be part of the wedding. It was going to be the wedding of the decade, but there was other news. The church family had moved into a new sanctuary and Tresa's sister had given birth to her first baby. Tresa was the last daughter of the pastor to be given away in marriage. What a happy year for the entire family!

NOTES FOR THE READER

CHAPTER 4

MIXED EMOTIONS

It was about six weeks from the day of the wedding and Tresa was about to order the invitations when Paul started acting strange. He called Tresa at her job and told her that he wanted to call off the wedding. Tresa was furious! She went to her manager and told her that she didn't feel well, that she could only work half a day and she was then going home because she was sick. She left and after she got into her car, she removed the ring, placing it in the ashtray. She drove off in a rage.

When she arrived at the place her mom worked, she went to the front but her Father, who was in the midst of a meeting, answered the door. Although her eyes were filled with tears, she didn't want to say anything that would embarrass either of them so she just asked where her mother was. He told her and she walked down the hall with tears running down her face. When her mother saw her, she could feel Tresa's pain, and her mother embraced her.

Tresa set up a meeting for her and Paul with her father, who was not only their counselor but also their Pastor.

"One day you want to be married and the following day, you don't," began her father. "What's going on?"

Paul replied, but he only gave them information about his family. The Pastor said, "Now, Paul, it's either your family or Tresa. Family is always going to be there, but Tresa is going to be your wife. She will be your new family."

So Paul decided that he wanted Tresa more than he wanted to be with his family.

The day of Tresa's Bridal Shower arrived. She was very nervous because she didn't know what to expect. She didn't have anything appropriate to wear, so a few hours before the shower was to begin she went to Gantos Boutique, which was located approximately 30 minutes from her home. She knew she had no time to spare because the traffic was heavy and there were many detours. She was afraid that she would be late for her own shower. Plans were on the roll.

Time passed quickly and before she knew it, it was the day of her wedding. After she woke up she went to her sister's home to get her hair done. She was still glowing, still very excited, not the least bit nervous. Tresa's sister was happy for her 'cause she knew that Tresa needed this big thing to happen to her because heretofore she had always had bad experiences in her relationships. Tresa's heart went out to her sister. By the time she left her sister's home, she was excited again.

She went to the mall to get her ring polished. She had an appointment to have her face made up at Hudson's and she made it on time. After Tresa arrived and sat down, the lady started applying makeup. She received many compliments on her appearance; everyone told her that she would make a beautiful bride. She left Hudson's drove to where they were holding her bridal shower, arriving on time. There were many chairs and tables and many game gifts. She was humbled because so many people had attended. Although people had always appeared to be uninterested in her, she now felt that they must have some affection for her. Prior to this, only her immediate family, her parents and her sister, had treated her this lovingly.

By the time the shower began, there were over 150 people in attendance. This made her want to cry but she didn't want to ruin her makeup or have her mascara run. She received numerous compliments and many gifts, gags and encouraging words. People who really hadn't paid attention to her before were showing their kindness and support. Inside, Tresa was thanking God for sending so many people to bless her.

After the shower, Tresa went to Taco Bell and had a Mexican pizza and then she went to church. She was so nervous that she was crying and smiling at the same time. Finally, the girls who were going to be in her wedding, along with her new mother-in-law, approached her. They made Tresa sit down and relax. She wanted to help the girls get dressed but she couldn't relax long enough to do this.

NOTES FOR THE READER

CHAPTER 5

THE BIG DAY

It was finally time for Tresa to put on her wedding dress. Her mother was assisting her and Tresa's could tell by the look in her mother's eyes that she was proud of her daughter and very happy for her. Since her mother was the wedding corrindator, many people knocked on the door and asked her to help them accomplish their part in the wedding. This made her mother nervous, and she finally became so agitated with the interruptions that Tresa had to laugh.

The photographer arrived and it was time to take photographs of the bridal party.

Tresa's grandfather was going to walk with her down the aisle and give her away, since her father was going to perform the ceremony. Her grandfather came into the room and told her how proud he was of her and that she was beautiful; they both began to cry. Tresa managed to go to the door where the greeters were, and she heard their exclamations of oohs and aahs, one after the other. The usher instructed Tresa that her queue to enter was when the music started playing. Tresa replied that she really loved the song now playing and she told everyone to wait a minute so

24

the whole song could be played while she was walking through the doors and down the aisle. When she walked in, everyone stood up in awe. Many people didn't recognize her. She received many compliments as she walked down the aisle; she was speechless.

The church was filled; there was even an overflow of people into the balcony. There were approximately 1,100 people at the church with about 600 persons attending her wedding. Tresa couldn't believe that on the biggest day of her life, the church was packed and all those people were there to support her.

Once the ceremony was over and all the photographs had been taken, Paul and Tresa went to their home and started going through their wedding gifts and the cash and checks that had been given to them. All of the house warming gifts would remain in a room at the church until they returned from their two-week honeymoon. They changed clothing and put their luggage into the back of Tresa's car, then went to a post-wedding celebration which the out-of-town guests and a few close family members were going to attend. Tresa's smile was still glowing.

Later, they went over to the home of one of Paul's relative's, where they received more gifts as well as monetary offerings. Some photographs were taken before they left.

They then went to the gas station and filled up and after that, they were then on the road, on their honeymoon. Paul drove for many hours and didn't rest until they were just outside his home state. They stayed in a motel, where they slept for about seven hours.

Once awake, they were soon on the road again but Tresa slept almost the entire day.

Their destination was Myrtle Beach, South Carolina. They arrived at their hotel, which was on one of the beaches along the shore of the Atlantic Ocean.

Tresa had the time of her life. They were like children. They went shopping and saw some movies, and went to different amusement parks. One evening they went to a video game and pool table parlor, and they stayed really late. They walked the boardwalk, ate at a seafood restaurant and rented movies. They also attended different shows – medieval horse shows featuring southern belles as singers and dancers.

Not only were these shows great entertainment, they also served five-course meals.

Towards the end of the week they headed toward Paul's home town, approximately six hours from Myrtle Beach. Tresa was apprehensive about meeting his family because she didn't know how they would accept her. First, she met Paul's sister, who owned her own home. They stayed a few nights there, and his sister loved Tresa as if she were her own sister. By the time they arrived at Paul's grandparent's home.

Tresa felt like part of the family. She had met his grandparents the year before at Paul's aunt's house during the Thanksgiving holiday. Later, Tresa met the rest of the family, whom she loved.

Tresa was homesick and she suggested that on the way back, they go by her sister's home in Missouri, so they were off. Paul asked Tresa to drive, but she couldn't handle it.

The traffic made her nervous and they were driving through Kentucky, where everything was unfamiliar.

When they arrived, Tresa was very happy to see her sister again. She felt like she was finally at a place where she had something in common with the people. Tresa thought that Paul's attitude was weird and she told her sister this. She had noticed this change of attitude while they were visiting his home town, after he had had a couple of drinks, but since they were on their honeymoon, she thought it was probably alright.

Still, it had bothered her.

NOTES FOR THE READER

CHAPTER 6

REALITY SETS IN

Once Tresa and Paul were on their way home to the real world, Paul started snapping at Tresa for little things. If it wasn't the way she was driving or the way she was dressed, it was her personality. Just little things, but it really bothered her.

One evening at the dinner table, Paul told her that she couldn't always run back to her parents when things weren't going right between them, and Tresa started to cry.

"When you make such remarks, it really hurts," she said.

"You need to grow up," he replied.

Tresa remained silent.

Before another month had passed, Paul began working at his midnight shift job.

"It's time for me to start my second job," he explained. Tresa became very angry and told him that

29

he should stay home with her at night and they could both work during the day.

"I can't stand for you to be up under me all the time," he replied. That statement <u>really</u> hurt! It made her feel like her own husband didn't want to be around her.

When Paul wanted to go out, he always came up with an excuse but Tresa felt that he just wanted to be away from her. Once, when Tresa was hungry, Paul told her to go to Taco Bell and get them something to eat. When she said that she was afraid to drive at night, he snapped at her and said, "Well, I will go."

"I'll go with you," she said.

"It's only down the street," he replied.

She thought, "Why is it that he always wants to go out by himself, especially when we are one now? In his mind he is still a single man, doing things, coming and going, and because he's a grown man he doesn't think anyone else needs to know his whereabouts, or what he does." Tresa didn't like that at all; it was if she were left out of everything. She felt like he was hiding something. He never wanted to talk to her.

One morning as Tresa was dressing to go to work, Paul rushed her out of the house.

When she came home that night, he took her into their bedroom and started yelling at her because she when she had gotten dressed that morning, she had left a panty-liner wrapped in toilet paper on the bed. Paul claimed that he was having open house visits for his friends and one friend saw the ball of tissue paper and also the yellowed paper that hung on Tresa's closet door. This was a prayer to God and an eye-opener to Paul about Holy living and how a wife should be treated, according to the Bible. Paul said his friend had asked him if he were back into the world, and he was embarrassed.

"How can you have people walk through our home without straightening up first?" she asked. He didn't care, he said, and started yelling at her, making nasty and unpleasant comments. He repeatedly stated that woman at his job were always asking him why his wife didn't clean and cook for him.

"Why did we get married if I have to do everything for myself?" he asked. "You can't do anything right." Then he used verbal threats and made more evil remarks.

On another morning as Tresa was getting dressed for work, she noticed that Paul had taken her car and left her stranded. She called Paul's midnight job to see if he had left work yet and the lady who answered told her that Paul hadn't been at work. Tresa was furious! She paged Paul several times but he didn't respond. Finally, he came home and, raising his voice, he told her to get into the car and go to work. Tresa questioned him and he said only that he couldn't leave his job early to take her to work. She then told him that she had called his job, and he had not been at work. Tresa could smell alcohol on his breath, so she knew that he had been drinking.

On many occasions after Tresa had left the house to go to Friday night prayer service, Paul would leave and stay out all not, not returning home until Saturday morning. Tresa, who would cry for hours, began to have severe headaches.

One night she called Paul's cousin's wife, who told her that her car was parked outside their house. She explained that Paul had been stone drunk, too drunk to drive, so they had driven him over to their house and parked her car outside their door. He was evidently out of it. The only way his cousin knew that Paul didn't go home to Tresa was because she could hear his pager going off. Then she could hear Paul call and curse Tresa out for paging him.

The following Friday night, Tresa asked Paul to take her out. He told her that after she came back from prayer, they would go to a movie. He told her that he couldn't go to prayer because he had received a phone call from his job and that he had to go to a meeting at 6 pm.

"After the meeting, there won't be time," he said. After he left, Tresa checked the answering machine and heard the message about Paul's meeting. It was Paul's voice on the machine, disguised. She couldn't believe that her husband had lied to her.

NOTES FOR THE READER

_____

_____

_____

_____

_____

_____

_____

_____

_____

_____

_____

_____

_____

_____

_____

_____

_____

_____

_____

_____

_____

_____

_____

CHAPTER 7

THE GREAT SEPARATION

Paul started working late shifts and spending less and less time with Tresa. After he picked her up from work, he would lay down on the couch and watch *Divorce Court* and other shows on TV until time for his second job to start. Tresa wanted them to do things together, but he always stressed the fact that he worked two jobs and told her her was entitled to his rest. He would throw in her face conversations with other women about her not making his lunch, and how she didn't do this or that for him. When he came home, he complained to her about the things she did and didn't do, and talked about how her wanting a husband but, he said, she wasn't ready for one 'cause she didn't cook or clean.

"Everything that is done," he said, "I did for myself before we got married. What is the use of being married if can't do the things that I've been doing for myself?" She was very hurt. Paul began to say things that cut deeply into her soul.

She would go to church with a smile on her face and when Paul was around, people would ask, "How's married life? Are you still happy?" Things like that.

She lied to them because she wanted the world to think that she was happy. There were many nights when Paul told her how happy he had been before she came into his life. Those were serious words, and they tore Tresa to pieces.

It was Thanksgiving, their first together, and Paul suggested that they go out of town to see his family. Tresa didn't really want to go, but since she wanted to be with her new husband and she had no more vacation time, she went to her place of employment and lied to them. She told her manager that her husband had bought her a plane ticket and it was non-refundable, and since she had no more vacation time, she because she really wanted to be at home with her parents.

NOTES FOR THE AUTHOR

CHAPTER 8

THE SECRET IS OUT

They drove Tresa's car down south and stayed with Paul's grandparents on his mother's side. Tresa liked them. After they had been there for a few nights nights, they double dated with Paul's brother and his wife. The women liked each other and became good friends. Later, Paul and Tresa stayed at his sister's home and Tresa met his sister's boyfriend. They all went to the movies. Then Paul decided that he wanted to go out with his cousins so he left Tresa alone at his sister's house.

When Paul took Tresa to his other grandparent's home, his father's parents, and also to his aunt's home, he again left her alone with the women and took off in Tresa's car.

This time he went on a drinking and partying spree. This upset her so much she vomited and she began to feel very sick. One night during a visit to Paul's sister house, he didn't come home, all night. Tresa spent the night in the bathroom, vomiting and crying. Paul came home really late, stone drunk. After he entered the house he began talking in a very loud voice, cursing and swearing at his sister and his cousins, telling them that he didn't have to explain his wherabouts to Tresa.

"I'm a grown man!" he said. Tresa wasn't asleep; she heard every word he said. She didn't know what to do. She had never seen Paul in this state of mind. She was very hurt and the tears flowed freely down her face until she finally dozed off.

The day after his grandparents wedding anniversary party, the entire family said that they were going to a club, a bar, just for fun. Paul suggested that they go, too. One of his cousin spoke up and said, "Paul, perhaps you should consult Tresa."

When Tresa looked at Paul, he said, "Let's go to the club, baby."

"I don't go to clubs and I don't compromise," Tresa replied, loudly. "I'm a Christian, in town or out of town."

Paul said, "We won't be going."

NOTES FOR THE READER

CHAPTER NINE

THE GREATEST HURT OF ALL

Paul, his cousin and his sister went back to their grandparents home. The men were drinking.

"Paul, I really need to talk to you," Tresa said. He snapped at her and yelled, "Go back into the house!" He was really drunk.

With tears running down her face, Tresa said, "Paul, you told me that drinking was a thing of the past. So, why are you drinking every night on our trip? You aren't spending any time with me and this is supposed to be our first holiday together."

He didn't seem to care. He started raging; his tone was very violent. Tresa told Paul how sick she had been feeling and that she was really depressed because of his behavior. Then she explained that she thought that she was pregnant.

Paul, in loud voice, said to an embarrassed Tresa, "You want me to put it all up on a flag that my wife is pregnant and you want me to pamper you."

Tresa ran to the car with tears, like a fountain, rolling down her face. It was as though Paul really didn't want to be married. She thought that perhaps he had married her because he wanted to prove to his family that he could get whoever he wanted. This made Tresa very angry and she left.

When his sister noticed that Tresa wasn't around, she began looking for her. She finally found Tresa in the car and she went up to the window. When she saw Tresa's face, she could tell that this time she was really devastated. Tresa explained that she had informed Paul that she was pregnant and he had brushed it off, like he wasn't the father. There were so many emotions trapped inside her but she didn't want to tell anyone how she felt. She was very depressed. Then Paul approached the car and told Tresa to stay with his sister, that he was going on a party hunt with his cousins, which made Tresa furious. She raised her voice, saying that no one was driving her car and that he had brought her all the way down there and was leaving her with people that she hardly knew. The next morning when Tresa woke up, she was nauseated and still depressed, and she began to cry again. She noticed that Paul's side of the bed had not been slept in. She went into the other room where Paul's sister and her son were sleeping. His cousin Sean, who was in another room, noticed Tresa's sadness.

Paul's sister took her son to the store for something and Sean started watching television. Tresa asked Sean where Paul was.

"He has gone over to our aunt's house," Sean replied.

"I wonder why he didn't take me with him," Tresa remarked, "or even tell me where he was going."

Paul's sister's boyfriend came by and asked if she needed anything and Tresa said, "Yes, I would like a pizza. Is there a place nearby that deliveres?"

He told her there was and gave her his pager and his phone number, in case she needed something else. They ordered a pizza and after it arrived, Sean sat down and ate with Tresa.

Paul called at about 2 a.m. and Sean handed the phone to Tresa. She answered and Paul explained where he was, then told her he was going to take her to dinner and to the carnival that evening. The carnival was the best thing in town but Tresa was still sick, not to mention the fact that she was furious with Paul.

When it was time to return home, Paul's mother and aunt decided to go with them. After much preparation, they were finally on their way. The two women noticed how sick Tresa was and told Paul that he looked as if he'd been drinking throughout the entire trip, and his Mom was very upset with him for the way he had been acting.

NOTES FOR THE READER

CHAPTER TEN

LIES AND DECEIT

After they returned home, Paul began leaving the house early to go to work but Tresa soon found out that it wasn't work he was going to. Messages were left on the answering machine saying that he had to attend a meeting at work and the caller didn't know how long the meeting was going to be. Once again, the voice sounded just like her husband's.

Paul started hanging out in the streets after work and he didn't come home in the morning; when he did go home, he was in drunk. Following these drinking bouts, he missed work and if it was Sunday, he wouldn't go to church. Many times when Paul stayed out drinking on Saturday night, Tresa wouldn't attend church services on Sunday because she was too embarrassed to go to church without him. When she did go, she would find herself sitting there, crying.

Many times when she got home from work on Friday night Paul would be lying down, watching television. He refused to attend prayer meeting. He told Tresa to bring a tape back from church services and they could go somewhere after she got home. She would rush out of the church after prayer meeting and return to an empty house. Paul would be on partying.

If she called him on his Nextel walkie-talkie phone and asked him how long he was going to be, he would never tell her the truth. She would dress in her new lingerie for him, light candles and put on perfume and he wouldn't even show. She would end up crying herself to sleep. If he did come home, it wasn't until 4 am or 5 am the following morning.

Many times when Tresa called him he cursed her, saying, "When I come home, you'll know it! Now stop calling me, and don't page me again." While they were on the phone, many times Tresa would hear his friends in the background, remarking that they couldn't believe how he was talking to his wife. That would hurt and she would cry even more. This became a routine; every week the same thing would happen, over and over again.

One day near Christmas, Tresa was decorating their home for the holiday when Paul told her that she needed to clean up because his aunt was coming to stay with them. This upset her because it was always all about his family. He showed more enthusiasm about his aunt and his other family members than he did about her.

She often found herself in an argument with him over his drinking. This became a daily occurrence. Tresa hated arguing, but he aggravated her more each day. She would play the bible study tapes on *Living Right* and listened to how a Christian marriage should be while she was ironing his clothes. Paul sometimes came home and he would hear these tapes; she hoped that he was listening to the words. Tresa prayed for Paul to change his lifestyle; instead, everything seemed to deteriorate even more.

Tresa's friend and her husband visited them almost every day. At first, she thought this was cool but their visits soon began to get on her nerves. It was like her friend's husband spent more time with Paul than Tresa did. Paul asked Tresa what was wrong with her because she seemed to be sick all the time. Tresa always gave him an excuse.

It was the week of the Christmas holiday and on Christmas Eve there was a party at Tresa's place of employment. She asked Paul for money to buy her employer a gift. He explained that he had no money and said they should keep their money for Y2K. She felt like a poor woman at a Blue Light Special at Kmart when she couldn't buy anything. Tresa began borrowing money from her sister and her cousin so she wouldn't appear to be so poor.

The following week, Tresa's friend and her husband cooked a meal for her, Paul and her brother. Tresa's brother planned to spend the night with them but Paul didn't come home 'til late. Her brother went home without seeing Paul, who had called twice to explain that he was in another city but he said he was on his way. Tresa's friend's husband took the phone and Paul asked him to get some money out of their spare bedroom and go buy whatever food was needed for dinner. That's how Tresa found out about Paul's money stash.

Later, Paul told her that this money was for hard times. Tresa said she couldn't believe that Paul had acted like they were poor when he had a stash of money hidden from her.

Later, Paul planned to have dinner with Tresa, her friend and her friend's husband but again, he didn't show up. He had been gone the entire day, even though when he left he had explained to them that he wasn't going to be gone long. About 30 minutes before Paul arrived Tresa packed her bags, telling her guests that she was tired of living like this.

"This isn't love," she said, "it's deserting and neglecting."

Her friend's husband told her that he would talk to Paul and that she shouldn't leave him.

He said, "A man has his pride."

Paul came home about midnight, just before time for him to go to work. Tresa told him that her brothers hadn't been able to spend even one day with their new brother-in-law, or have a meal with him.

"I'm sorry," Paul said. "I'll make it up to them later." He then said that he and his friend were going out to pick up some movies and that they would be right back.

"Paul, aren't you going to work?" Tresa asked.

"Oh! Bye, everyone! See you later, Tresa."

Once again, she cried herself to sleep. Crying was a big part of Tresa's life. Her Mom called often to check on her and her sister and her dad realized that often, Tresa was crying while she spoke with them on the phone. She was in serious pain. She felt neglected, misused and verbally abused.

Apparently, Paul never knew.

NOTES FOR THE READER

CHAPTER ELEVEN

THE GREAT ESCAPE

It was Christmas Eve, Paul got in from work at about 3 am and went to sleep. At 9 a.m. the phone rang; he got up and got dressed. When Tresa saw that he was going out, she asked him why was he leaving. He explained to her that his aunt wanted him to go shopping with her. He then told her to clean the house because they were going to have company that night.

Tresa cleaned the house and sat around waiting for him until she was bored. Paul finally called and told her that he was outside switching cars, that he was going back to the mall and that she should go to her parent's house. After she arrived at her parents, she began to wonder why she was alone on Christmas eve. It was late when she left to go home. After she arrived she waited for Paul, but he didn't show up. Once again, she cried herself to sleep.

Her sleep was troubled and when she rolled over in the middle of the night, she noticed that Paul still wasn't home. Then she heard her cell phone ringing. It was Paul's cousin, paging him on her phone. She answered, but no one replied. She called the number back but Paul's cousin said he didn't know where her husband was.

When Tresa got up next morning, she was really angry! She had finally gotten tired of being last on Paul's list. She started talking out loud to herself while she put her belongings into her car. In her fury, alligator tears were rolling down her cheeks. She kept telling herself that it was all about his aunt and his family, and he couldn't even spend the holidays with his own wife. It took Tresa all of 20 minutes to put the majority of her belongings into the car; it had taken her about four weeks to move everything in.

Her anger intensified as she drove home. She called Paul's mother, who was down South.

Then she called her parents to ask if she could return to their home to live. She explained that Paul hadn't been at home the day before. When she arrived, her parents opened their arms wide to receive her, as if she were the prodigal daughter. She moved back into her old room and cried for hours. Her mom stayed with her, building her up and comforting her soul.

She stayed with Tresa until she fell asleep.

A few hours later, the phone rang; it was Paul. Tresa's father spoke to him and he said he was concerned about his wife, wondering where she was. But he didn't come and get her.

NOTES FOR THE READER

CHAPTER TWELVE

TORTURE AND TERROR

Tresa was confused. She was still sick and she couldn't eat. She was depressed and she didn't want to be bothered with anything. Her mother was there for her, supporting her through her misery. Tresa cried from morning 'til night. It was as though she were a manic depressive. There was no laughter in her heart; her spirit was in mourning. She was usually a cheerful person but she found that now, she couldn't smile.

One week passed. Paul may have missed her but he was very angry with her for leaving.

Her confusion continued. She wanted to go back to him and she wanted to hear him say, "Come back!" But he would only say, "You are the one who left."

Paul told Tresa that he didn't want to be married anymore. He informed her that he didn't think that he had ever had loved her. She was devastated. She didn't know how to react to this. In the end the decision was made between them to separate, and Tresa filed for divorce.

Paul was served his divorce papers but he didn't sign them. Instead, he began to harrass her.

He gave her so much trouble and distressed her so much that, many times, she didn't know if she were going or coming.

Tresa had left the Christmas gifts for Paul at his house. With a friend, she drove over to pick up some of the things that she had left there. As she was entering his driveway, Paul called her on the cell phone and told her to come to the back door to get her stuff – he had placed her belongings between the wooden door and the screen door. It was very cold outside and Tresa couldn't believe how mean Paul was treating her. While she was still at the back of the house, Paul flashed the gifts that he had purchased for Tresa, to show her friend. He told Tresa that he had bought her a cashmere coat and a Coach bag, along with a pair of diamond earrings that she wanted but that she didn't deserve any of these things because she had left him.

This nightmare went on for weeks. Finally, Tresa met with her attorney. She was confused and undecided, not knowing whether she really wanted to divorce Paul. She wanted to wait to see if he would change his mind. She really loved him, but his attitude had pushed her away.

Tresa had put her name on the furniture in the home that they had shared and Paul was not paying for it, or for some of the other bills. This was a messy situation. Finally, after calling Tresa where she worked, Paul gave her half of what they owed on the furniture. Tresa was satisfied, even though she felt that he should have given her twice the money he actually paid her. She decided to call it even. Paul kept the furniture and she received the wedding ring.

The divorce was soon finalized. Now she could begin her life all over again.

NOTES FOR THE READER

CHAPTER THIRTEEN

GOD IS TURNING IT ALL AROUND

Tresa prayed night and day, asking God to give her back the joy that she had once felt, and to give her the strength to make it through this nightmare. She could never have imagined that such sorrow could be the result of saying I do. Those two words are very powerful.

One year from the date of Tresa's bridal shower she had a terrible dream, with flashbacks, involving her and her ex-husband. She woke up crying, wondering why she had had this dream. Once again, she cried herself to sleep. The following day, which was Sunday, Tresa went to church and enjoyed the choir's singing. She praised the Lord. She really felt that the choir was ministering to her with music. The songs that touched her deeply were, "Won't Turn Back", "Your Grace and Mercy" and "Through It All". These songs brought tears to her eyes. Tresa remembered that this was the anniversary of her bridal shower, when she had wept tears of joy; now those tears had turned into tears of sorrow. Tresa couldn't really stop weeping; the tears flowed like a fountain from her eyes. She noticed that her aunt was at the service and she asked her aunt to follow her to the powder room. Her aunt asked Tresa if everything was alright and Tresa began crying even harder. She explained about the nightmare she had had the night before, and that it would soon be a year since she had said "I DO." She also stated that she felt that she wasn't a good role model because she had let everyone down.

Tresa's aunt stopped her and told her that she felt that something would have been wrong with Tresa if she hadn't shown her pain during this past year.

"Since all of this trauma," said her aunt, "you haven't shown any emotion. We thought there was something wrong with you because you held everything in, for such a long time.

"You're finally breaking down that wall; you can no longer pretend that everything is all right. You are finally facing it head on."

She encouraged Tresa for 20 minutes and then they went back into the sanctuary. Tresa felt better, but she was light headed. She thought that maybe she was dehydrated, 'cause she had cried all the night before and here she was, crying again.

On Monday, the Lord spoke to Tresa's heart about Paul's cousin. Tresa remembered that she had blamed the problems in her marriage on his cousin because he saw Paul more frequently than she did, even when they were newlyweds. Tresa decided to ask him to forgive her so after the church service, she spoke to his wife and just causally spoke to Paul's cousin.

When they drove off, the Lord reminded Tresa that she hadn't told Paul's cousin how she felt, so she began to pray and out of her mouth came the words confessing her forgiveness of the wrong that Paul had done to her in the past. She asked God to forgive him for the things he had done to her. When this was over, Tresa felt free; still, she knew what she had to do. So after Bible Class on Wednesday, she saw Paul's cousin's wife and explained to her that she had to speak with him, and why.

"We were talking about you just this morning," his wife said, and she told Tresa that he thought she should know he had nothing to do with the breakup of her marriage.

"What a coincidence," Tresa replied. She was about to let him know that she had forgiven him and that all of her problems with Paul had nothing to do with him and that it wasn't his fault, it was Paul's. Tresa told him all that was in her heart. They spent more than an hour talking and when they parted, Tresa felt a lightness in her being, in her step and in her heart, like a chain had broken. Forgiveness was in place.

Just like the scriptures say, "For whom the Son sets free is free indeed." Since that night, Tresa hasn't wept a tear or had any bad memories of her relationship with Paul.

After that incident, Tresa went to the Single's Fellowship at a restaurant. She was nervous because she felt that others were starring at her, perhaps thinking that she wasn't single. But she was free from it all; she felt that it was time to give her testimony about how God had brought her out of her misery and had restored joy to her heart. She had meant to give a 20 minute speech but it turned into an hour and thirty minutes. When she had finished, some who were there came up to Tresa and told her that she had given their own testimony but that they had been too scared to tell others. They went on to say that they were glad that Tresa had had the courage to come forth and share her testimony, and that it was a blessing to them all.

Tresa also had a great testimony concerning her job. She worked for a good company but when she asked her manager if she were to acquire an associate's degree, would the company compensate her for it. The answer was no and Tresa knew that it was time to leave. She was already working part-time at another establishment, so she went to the manager of that company and requested full-time hours, but on a part-time status.

Tresa couldn't believe the great move that she was making at that time. She quit the full- time job and enjoyed what she was doing at her other job. Within a short time a third facility made her an offer for a full-time position, with benefits and better pay. Tresa explained to upper management at the job where she currently worked, and they were not pleased at all.

After Tresa had had a physical at the third company, she had a meeting with two of the managers where she was currently working and they explained to Tresa that one of the physician's had given her a great performance review and they told her it was a shame to let such a good employee leave. They also said that they thought she should be given her what she wanted and proposed that Tresa work full-time, with benefits and a better salary than the third facility had offered, plus shift premium pay. Tresa was so pleased she could have cried.

She accepted their offer and she praised God daily.

The doctors, patients and Tresa's co-workers often complimented her on her work. She realized that only God could have turned a win-lose situation around so that it would work out in her favor. She prayed that God would turn the tables, and He had done so.

Tresa plans to stay in the healing process. She still attends church regularly, staying under the Word of God. Occasionally the musician at the church, her sister, plays the shouting song and Tresa remembers how far the Lord has brought her, and that he's changed her mourning into a joyful dance.

Tresa graduated from Northwood University in May 2001, with an Associate Degree in Business Management. She did not stop at that; the following May 2002, she graduated from Northwood University with a Bachelor's Degree in Business Management. She was on the Honor Roll.

Through everything that has happened in her life, she wrote three poems and submitted them to Poetry.com. All of them became winners and are being published this year. She received two "Editor's Choice "awards from the International Poets of America. Also, she wrote a biography for her school's portfolio and it was forwarded to the National Dean's List. It is being published and they have requested a photo and a short story of her life.

Tresa gives God all of the praise and glory. He has brought her through so many trials.

NOTES FOR THE READER

CHAPTER FOURTEEN

VICTORY IN THE NAME

No one could have known how much grief and pain Tresa had to endure during her marriage and after it was over. Paul took Tresa through so much, and never would she have guessed that she would have been able to tolerate it - only through the grace of God! She received her report card every two months and dedicated the rewards to God, because all things are possible through him. The National's Dean's List wrote a letter stating that they were honoring Tresa for being one of the top students in the one of the nation's finest schools. God is so good and is worthy of all praise and glory.

Tresa was accepted into the University of Missouri-St. Louis. She plans to go to school for her Masters in Management Information Specialist (MIS), now that she has a double minor in Journalism and Business Management from Northwood University.

While Tresa was excited at the thought of starting her life over, going to St. Louis to school and accomplishing her dream, she had mixed emotions that invaded her thoughts day and night. She kept her many troubles and worries inside, however. She was stressed, and so confused in every way possible, regarding school. The thought of moving to unfamiliar territory was stressful, and she had a fear of beginning again and achieving that which she had always dreamed about. It was fear of failing. It was fear of being rejected by people who loved her.

You see, Tresa had found a friend, a young man who lived a few miles from the school that she was to attend – the University of Missouri at St. Louis. This young man gave her so much inspiration and so many promising dreams, and he encouraged her to strive to accomplish her goal. After all that was said to her by this young man, Tresa began to imagine that she would never be lonely again. Perhaps she had finally met the man of her dreams, one who knew all the right words to say to her, which compliments to give her that would comfort her and assure her that he would always be there for her after graduation.

These dreams were rehearsed in Tresa's head, over and over again. She believed him, and she knew that he meant well. He always spoke in parables, as though he were practicing to be a Psychologist, and Tresa was a patient. She felt deep in her heart that this man really, truly loved her but their relationship was very strange, 'cause they never went out and had not yet gotten to know each other, the real people that they actually were.

Tresa believed in this guy but after some months, he was so preoccupied with finishing college and he took on such a heavy load of courses that his own life and his schoolwork became his main concerns and she was no longer a priority. This hurt her. It was like a repeat of what she had just been through, like it was happening all over again. Tresa didn't want to experience this same hurt, but it seemed that no matter how hard she tried not to fall into men's emotional traps, deep down in her heart she always did.

She may never tell her friend that, though, because after many emails, phone calls and letters, Tresa gave up. She didn't want him to think that she was harassing him. He had pursued her until she fell for him and then he had backed off.

Tresa stepped back from this emotional picture so she could stop and think. What is this man really attracted to? Is he pursuing me so he'll never have to worry about being alone?

Was he being honest with her? Was this true love or was it false hope? Who will ever know? Well, she didn't blame him, she blamed herself.

Time passed and Tresa spoke often with this man, and sometimes she would be upset with him for not returning her phone calls or not answering her letters. This was a time when she really needed a friend and a listening ear, but he was nowhere to be found. She began to pray, to talk to the Lord. She didn't want to lose focus; she wanted to understand herself.

She asked herself why she planned to go away to school. Time was flying by so fast and it was soon time to register for class, so Tresa was faced with a great decision, one that could change her life. It was time to reserve a seat on the airplane.

After much thought, she decided to stay home and attend a local university. She said this aloud and without really thinking about her reasons for this decision, she is suddenly at peace. But then, because of her sudden outburst, she is confused again. She was told that her sister planned to relocate to whereever she decided to go to school, and that since she thought that she would be attending UMSL, her sister had already moved there. Tresa took all of this information to heart as she is getting dressed to go to class. She was on her way to school when all of a sudden, tears stung her eyelids and she began singing one of her favorite artist's songs, Yolanda Adams, *"Open Heart"*. This song was ministering to her, helping her relieve the tension. The words tell her that she is afraid of making the wrong decision and that it may not be pleasing to God (paraphrasing). She begins singing to herself. After the song ends, she fast-forwards the track to *"Already Alright"*. She enjoys listening to this CD and as she approaches school, she wipes the tears, parks her car and gets her bags out and heads to class. She's trying to focus on positive things and trying to suppress her confusion, the sudden change caused by the decision that she had made that morning. Well, it isn't working out as planned.

Tresa is in the midst of writing a paper when tears again begin forming in her eyes. She rushes out and goes to the restroom, saying to herself, "You're going to be alright." After the break, she goes to work and tries to feel at peace again. She knows that her final decision will be made before her shift is over. She runs to her manager's office and begins discussing her indecision. Her boss encourages her and tells her that she's an inspiration to others, that she is very bright and a hard worker. She already knows these things; still, she needed to hear them at this time, at this hour. Again, she wanted to cry but she held back her tears.

As she was leaving she saw her friend, Pedro. She greeted him and began talking to him.

He encouraged her and built up her self-esteem - more than he will ever know. She really felt good after he had spoken with her, and she thanked him for his kind words.

After she arrived home, Tresa thinks back over her long, exhausting day. She wonders why she is feeling so much pain and anxiety. Then it all comes to her – she feels that she is letting her parents down because if she changes her plans and doesn't go to a top university, it would hurt her them. The feeling of disappointing them is crushing her. She also thought that her future may be altered because she would never have the opportunity to get to know the young man who loved her, the student who lived near UMSL and finally, she relived the rush that she had felt when completing all of the required classes, and working to keep her grade point average up so that she could graduate with honors, and then her graduation. It all came flooding back into her thoughts, and she went over these events again and again. She wondered why everything seemed to be a burden and she felt a slight depression that only came when she was alone, away from everyone. That night Tresa found herself in her bedroom with tears rolling down her cheeks, praying to her heavenly Father:

"Father in heaven, I come to you in a state of repentance. Lord, I've tried so hard to make my dreams come true that I didn't involve you in the decision, but I wanted you to bless it one hundred fold. Lord, I am sorry. I know that your word states, 'Many are the plans of the righteous but it's the Lord's purpose that shall stand.' I've wanted so badly to make my dreams come true, to be one who had been nothing and to become somebody overnight.

I was planning on moving away from my parents, family and friends. I am someone who tried to fit the pieces of my puzzling life into the right perspective, instead of bringing my life to you and having you make me over.

Lord, I've been hurt over and over again, and maybe it's my fault. I've allowed people to come in and try to give me a happy ending, but I did not allow you to do this, in your time.

Your word says that the 'Steps of a good man are ordered of the Lord.'

"Lord, I need you to order my steps. Show me the plans that you have for my life.

Guide my footsteps; give me, day by day, my daily bread. I don't want to hinder others by my actions. I don't want to try to fit in with others' plans, but only with your plans. I'll walk in your path and the person whom I need to meet, whom I will spend the rest of my life with, will be in my path and it will be up to me to choose him.

"Lord, show me where you want me to be. I know that going back to college and earning a degree is my choice. I just don't want to leave this place, the church that you've set me into, to get that degree and the job that you have for me. I wanted to start my life over but since my divorce, Lord, you've started my life over and you're working on me day and night. I may not notice it or even see it, but I know in my heart that I am 'under construction'. I think that the reason I wanted to leave is that I believed so much, in my heart and for such a long time, that I was proving something, that maybe if I were to move away for a few years, people would forget the mistakes that I've made in the past and when I was ready to come back, I would have a degree and be married and live happily ever after. But this is all that I wanted to do. I was going to throw away everything that I've worked for here - my good job, the new friends that I've made and the people whose lives I could have changed, the difference I could have made in their lives. The people who could come to Christ through me, during the time I am here.

"But I was giving all that up so that I could achieve my goals and dreams. Lord, I repent. I was being selfish and doing things to satisfy Tresa and not even getting counsel from you. I ask you to create in me a clean heart and to renew a right spirit in me. Lord, put people in my life that will not give me evil or ungodly counsel. One who will not lead me astray with words. Lord, I am not afraid because, 'God has not given me the spirit of fear but of Power, Love and a Sound Mind. Lord, I can do all things, through Christ who strengthens me. I thank you that my steps are ordered by you. Today, I will not live for Tresa, but for you."

After that prayer she slept. The following morning, she told her parents what was in her heart and they said that they were proud of her for going on to college and for having the determination to finish. Tresa started to cry again, and she informed her parents that she was going to register at a nearby university, here in her hometown, and go on to get her Bachelor's Degree in Computer Information Systems, and that she would continue to go to the school that she was currently attending and earn her Bachelor's Degree in Management.

NOTES FOR THE READER

CHAPTER 15

A WHOLE NEW OUTLOOK

Tresa's big day! She is turning a new age and she is so excited. Another day older; one more step toward maturity, trying not to make the same mistakes that caused her to stop moving forward. She woke up and looked in the mirror, wondering if she looked a year older. She dressed, prayed and thanked the Lord for one more day. She couldn't wait to get to work. She imagined the excitement with her coworkers. When she finally arrived at work, she couldn't wait to hear the cheers and congratulations.

She didn't feel that pride was causing her to be so excited; it was just that this was an accomplishment, like she had been waiting all year to conquer being that previous age and all of the toil and snares that she had had to overcome.

She saw her friend Pedro and they went to get coffee. She is so excited about her birthday and graduation that she can't hold all of the inspiring thoughts and feelings inside.

She is working hard, as usual, and is anticipating the end of her shift so that she will be able to finally relax and celebrate. She's had a difficult and very busy week. She completed a final exam in accounting and she worked hard at her job. So here she was, approaching the weekend. Besides being payday, the weekend was surely going to be a treat.

Tresa's cousin called and told her the time she expected to off work. Tresa wanted to go to this big-time restaurant that Pedro had suggested. After work she went home and Tresa's cousin called to tell her that she was waiting outside. She joined her cousin, was excited because they were going to hang out in the big city. Tresa and her cousin had an interesting conversation as they drove. They arrived at the restaurant shortly, and it was packed. When they entered, she noticed that the place was really nice. They ordered, and chatted while they waited for the food to arrive. Finally it did, and Tresa couldn't wait to enjoy the pasta and seafood. After dinner, she wanted to see the highlights of the city – she knew there was a fair and an art fest being held. She remembered that her friend, the one from out-of-state, had left her a message for her birthday and she thought that she should return his call. So she dialed his number and thanked him for contacting her. She really didn't want to get into an extensive conversation with him, she just wanted to thank him for calling. Their conversation made Tresa uncomfortable because he began talking about her moving to the city where he lived.

When Tresa was first going through her divorce, she wanted to escape the pain. She was still grieving during the time that she lived down south with her other sister and attended the university located there. It was then that she had became acquainted with this guy. There had been talk of marriage at the time, but it was all hypothetical. Then, after Tresa stopped thinking about him here he was again, suggesting that she move down there and start her life over. When she heard this, she assumed that it was leading to the end of their phone conversation, but it wasn't. Tresa didn't want her cousin to think that she was being rude, so she concluded the call by saying they would talk later that night.

Tresa came home from the long night of her birthday celebration and spoke to her father about their departure the following morning, and the long stretch until graduation. He told her they should leave early, by 8:30 am at the latest. This grieved Tresa because she was tired. She went to bed and tried to go to sleep. She had been asleep only for about an hour when the phone rang. It was her friend from down south, but Tresa had been in a deep sleep, so she asked him to call back later.

When she awoke on Saturday morning, she began pacing the floor and perspiring, wondering how she was supposed to react to this nerve-racking event. She tried to decide whether she had been more nervous on her wedding day or today, on her graduation day. She had butterflies in her stomach and perspiration was rolling down her arms and down her face.

She was terrified. They arrived 20 minutes before the group picture was going to be taken. Tresa and her father entered the building, not knowing where to find her cap and gown.

She had asked the ushers at the door, but they didn't have a clue. She became upset when the ushers didn't know where to find the caps and gowns, and she panicked. Her father noticed that Tresa was getting extremely nervous because she didn't want to miss the group graduation photo. He saw other graduates and asked them where the caps and gowns were being distributed. They had to walk quite a distance, or that is how it felt to Tresa.

Her counselor from school was there, one whom she hadn't seen in a long time. It was good to see a familiar face. The counselor helped Tresa put on her cap and gown. She was so nervous, she couldn't keep from crying.

It was time for the group photo. The sun was very hot that day. Her classmates were all making different gestures and silly comments to make the time go a little faster. Finally they were posed, the photo was taken and it was over. There was still approximately two hours before the actual processional was to begin. Tresa noticed that she was the only one in her program location with a gown that was a lighter shade than the others. She was a little embarrassed at first. Her father told her not to worry, people may just think that you're graduating with your Master's degree, so Tresa forgot about it.

Not only was she nervous, she was also very hungry. She didn't want to keep pacing in the sun, so she decided to try to find the buffet that was inside one of the buildings. She got a plate and chose wing dings, crackers and broccoli with ranch dressing. The food was good and so was the punch. Tresa thought that once she had eaten, some of the pressure would be relieved but it didn't help at all. She decided to go back and get some more food.

There was a seat available between two people she didn't know and Tresa asked if she could sit down. They began a conversation with her about school and their plans after graduation. They were very nice people. The graduate asked her why her gown was a different color from the others. She explained that she was graduating with an Associate's Degree and went on to say that it had been a truly a rough year for her, and she had decided that it was a great accomplishment and so she planned to march in this year's ceremony.

Time was going by really fast but they still had more than one hour to wait. The conversation with those people had helped, and she had made a friend on her graduation day.

The lady wanted Tresa to come outside with her and her family for a photo shoot. Tresa was grateful and she thought the lady was very kind to include her in their family photos. She even agreed to mail copies to her, which was nice of her.

It was time to line up. Tresa still didn't see a lot of light-colored gowns, but there were one or two. She was patiently waiting when suddenly a lady tapped her on the shoulder and told her that she was to march with her own group at the end of the line, so she went to the back of the line. She couldn't believe it! There were more than thirty graduates with the same color gown as hers. What a relief!

Well, this was the time that Tresa had been waiting for. The hour had arrived. The line started to form and they began to move into the gymnasium. Tresa was extremely nervous but she smiled because she could finally get out of the sun and into the shade. Once in the building she heard the strains of their graduation song, Tears formed in her eyes. Then she walked around the corner and noticed her father and mother. She didn't see her sister and brother-in-law and she wondered where they were.

The graduates lined up and said the Pledge of Allegiance to the American flag. That was nice. The place was packed. It was awesome, although a bit warm. Tresa overheard someone saying that there was no air conditioning, so this was going to be one warm event.

Finally the line she was in began to walk across the stage. Tresa heard family members calling her name and finally her sister, brother-in-law and niece showed up. When the lady called her name, Tresa didn't want to trip over her gown or stumble going up the stairs. (This is something that everyone prays doesn't happen to them in front of a lot of people, especially on graduation day). She shook the person's hand who was giving out the diploma, and posed twice for photos.

It was finally over; Tresa stopped perspiring. Now came the most boring time of all, listening to the end of the ceremony, knowing that her part was completed. Everyone in Tresa's family came one by one and asked her to leave. Tresa was hesitant; she didn't want to leave until the ceremony was over. Finally, after seeing her father, she ran out.

Everyone congratulated her as they started the family photo shoot. Her father explained that he wanted to leave early because once the ceremony was over and everyone was leaving, there would be a major traffic jam.

Tresa started thinking of her birthday/graduation party at the Hotel. She looked at the room number, etc. Her father took them home by the scenic route. Ha ha. They still arrived home by 6 pm, the time the party was to begin. Tresa got some snacks out for the party. Her father dropped her off so she could pick up her truck and be on her way. Once again, she was excited. She had finally completed the first degree towards her career. She went on to the hotel. Her phone rang three different times. Her guests at the hotel were calling;

they were waiting patiently, they said, so she explained that she was on her way.

When she arrived one of her friends told her that she had previous engagements and she left her card as she congratulated Tresa. So Tresa went on into the hotel, gathered all of her things, then headed up to the room. It was a beautiful suite. She changed into more comfortable clothing, then inserted the tape into the video player and picked up something to eat. She was exhausted. Her guests were mingling and eating. Then her sister called. She was with her niece. They were bringing the main course, the spaghetti. They arrived, and Tresa was happy to see her niece again.

After the video had played for hours everyone started leaving, one by one. Tresa thanked them all for coming. Her cousin was the last to leave. She had brought the ice cream cake, which was awesome. Finally, Tresa lay down and watched a couple of movies that were on television, then she fell asleep.

In the morning, she had to get ready for church. It was a beautiful Sunday morning. She had a little trouble carrying all of the things to the car so she called the front desk and asked them send someone up. It was truly a blessing that she didn't have to haul all of that down the hall. That would have been very difficult. After everything was loaded into her automobile, she inquired about breakfast. Even though she was still parked illegally, she took advantage of the hotel breakfast and had a bacon and egg sandwich before she left for the church.

This truly had been a blessed week for Tresa. She looked back and thought, God is so good and truly is faithful. She proclaimed that, "There is nothing too hard for God," and that "God is able to do exceeding, abundantly, above all that she could ask or think."

Tresa had developed a new outlook on life and she was now taking one day at a time, knowing that with God, all things are possible. And Tresa proclaimed daily, "All Blessings, Power and Might be to the only wise and true God who promotes his own. I love you, Jesus, and I thank you for giving me the opportunity to know you as a Lawyer in a courtroom, a healer, a mender of broken hearts, a restorer, omnipresent, Omnipotent, friend, comforter in the midnight hour and a bridge over troubled water. God is so good."

One year later, Tresa had made it through that long, frustrating year and had completed her undergraduate degree in Business Management.

She now has her Bachelor's Degree. God has opened another door in her life – she was offered a job at her church as Office Manger. Who says that God doesn't reward your faithfulness and isn't able to do exceedingly, abundantly, above all that you can ask or think.

Even though Tresa had received numerous persecutions on her previous job, she knew by those trials that blessings would be right around the corner. God was treating Tresa like he did Job in the bible. He was blessing her with double. More than she had had in the beginning – a Double Portion, so to speak, but she loved the Lord and she has dedicated it all back to him.

NOTES FOR THE READER

**TAKING A LOOK BACK OVER YOUR LIFE,
THINK THINGS OVER,
WRITE DOWN WHAT GOD HAS DONE FOR
YOU,
THEN WRITE DOWN HOW MANY INSTANCES
THAT YOU HAD
<u>TO COUNT IT ALL JOY</u>
THEN THINK, IF HE'S DONE IT BEFORE, HE'LL
DO IT AGAIN**

And Jesus looking upon them saith, With men it is impossile, but not with God: for with God all things are possible. (MARK 10:27)

HEY, IT'S TESTIMONY TIME!!!! TIME TO SHOUT AND PROCLAIM VICTORY IN EVERY AREA OF YOUR LIFE AND WATCH GOD MOVE ON YOUR SITUATIONS!!!!!!!!!!!!!!!!!!

1.

2.

3.

4.

5.

6.

7.

8.

9.

10.

11.

12.

13.

14.

15.

16.

17.

18.

19.

20.

21.

22.

23.

24.

25.

26.

27.

28.

29.

30.

31.

32.

33.

34.

35.

36.

37.

38.

39.

40.

THE MAN IN MY LIFE

I've sat alone, lonely and depressed, hoping that someone would rescue me from the hurts of this world. One day this man walked into my life and dried all my tears. He said: You want affection; I'll draw you with cords of love. When I come into your room, I will send warm feelings down your spine. You can call me whenever you need me. I'll bring you joy in sorrow and hope for tomorrow. When you're sick, I'll touch you and instantly the love I have for you will erase all the hurt and pain. I'll be the sunshine in your rainy life. I'll give you peace in all situations. I'll never leave you or forsake you; I'll never let you down; I'll erase your past and bring you great happiness. I'll never change; I will be the same yesterday, today, and forever. "I am Jesus. Open up your heart and let me in."

By Sandra L. Crump Walker
Copyright @2000

LOVING MY TRUE LOVE

From the first time we met, I could close my eyes and didn't have to see you to know that you were there. I feel your presence all the time. When I am afraid, you caress me with your love and you are always with me, letting me know that you'll never leave me or forsake me. You say that all things work together for my good. When I lay down to sleep, you always put a smile on my face. When I weep during the late hours, you wipe my tears and give me peace. If you need a true, unconditional love that, no matter what, will forgive you of all sins, you need to meet the man and lover of my soul. I would like to introduce to some and present to others, the man in my life: Jesus Christ.

By Sandra L. Crump
Copyright @2000

HE'S ALL THAT TO ME

Jesus is all of that to me. He's my friend, He's joy in sorrow.

He gives me continuous victory. He steps in, right on time. He supplies my needs. I dedicate all of my rewards and honors to Him, all to him, because he is worthy and is all of that to me.

By Sandra L Crump
Copyright @2000

Final Words from the Author, to you the

reader

***Serve God wholly and in everything. Don't try to help God out. Wait on him, allow him to help you in your relationships. If things are starting out badly, don't try making it good. If it's of God, it will all work out.

Take care and God bless. God is able to do exceeding, abundantly above all that you can ask or think. (Ephesians 3:20) and He that has begun a good work in you, will also perform it.(Philippians 1:6)

***I hope this book has been an inspiration and that my testimony has touched your heart.

Also, if you have been one of the ones who are quick to talk about the negativity in someone's life, take a look in your mirror and ask yourself if it were you who was going through something terrible and personal, how you would feel if others talked about your personal issues.

If God has brought me out and on top, he'll do the same for you. I love you all.

DEDICATION TO MY PARENTS

This message is dedicated to my parents, Earl and Earnestine Crump. I wrote this paper for my English class and I am not ashamed of these truths. My parents chose to include discipline in raising my brothers and sisters and believe me, it worked. We are the product of that discipline today and I just want to say thanks, I needed it.

While explaining what the performance of my parents means to me, I will explain the outcome of the person who has received discipline compared with one who hasn't.

My parents emphasized that if you wanted to train a child on how to live and how to behave in a certain way, you may discipline them within the first five years of their lives.

After this age, they'll be able to distinguish the difference between good and bad. Once a child knows the difference, a child is ready to receive discipline.

Just by being around my younger siblings and my sister's daughter, I've observed at least one thing that we all have in common: children know when they are doing right and wrong. When a child wants to get into something that they know is prohibited, they will look at their parents or the one who's left in charge; when they know or think that they can get away with doing whatever it is they want to do, they'll go forward with it. With their disciplinarian in the house, the child will surely suffer the consequence of his actions.

The scripture in the bible that is always set in stone in my family is, *Proverbs 22:6, "Train up a child in the way he should go and when he is old, he will not depart from it."* This scripture is so true. No matter what children have to face in their lifetime, if their parents took time to instill how to live and behave around people and the difference between right and wrong, then when the child is outside their parental boundaries, that child will not only show respect to those in authority, but it will be obvious that the parents of that child have taken the time to train the child in all aspects of life. Sometimes, the child may know that they are doing wrong but deep down inside, they will never leave what's right; they will always find themselves repeating, "What did my parents say about this?" or, "I remember that my parents told me not to do such a thing," etc.

Well, indeed, my parents always took the time to discipline my siblings and myself, as often as we needed it. My father says that children will let you know when they need chastisement because they will continue to do things that they are told not to do, and will watch to see how you will react to it.

I remember, many times I would act in a way that was very embarrassing to my mother and she would always reinforce this same thing to me, "I will, indeed, spank you when you get home and you must remind me to do so; if not, your punishment will be double."

To remind her was like taking a chance on your life but if you didn't and she remembered, then it's twice the punishment. While she chastised us, she would always use the scripture, *Proverbs 22:15, "Foolishness is bound in the heart of a child; but the rod of correction shall drive it far from him."* Now, it was bad enough that my parents spanked us but I think it was worse that they used the Word of God while doing it.

I've heard that some parents give a speech while they were chastise their children.

Example, "Did I not tell you so and so? You're not going to embarrass me, etc." I don't know which was worse, the spanking or the speech that went with it.

In my family, we refer to the Word of God in all aspects of life. During our discipline, one Quote that was used I remembered always during the time I was growing up. *Proverbs 29:17, "Correct thy son, and he shall give thee rest; yea, he shall give delight unto thy soul"*

*A*lso in the same chapter, *Proverbs 29:15, "The rod and reproof give wisdom: but a child left to himself bringeth his mother to shame."*

Just by understanding those passages of scripture and by attending school, it's easy to identify those who have been disciplined and those whose parents let the children go their own way. Those without chastisement bringeth their mother to shame. A good example is while at a store you often notice a child who seems to be out of his mother's control The mother doesn't discipline the child at all; when the child doesn't have his way, he starts a great commotion and draws a lot of attention, not necessarily always to himself but sometimes to his mother.

I will not boast about myself but I think that if I had not received the corrections that were due me at an early age and throughout the time of entering young adulthood, I probably would not be the person that I now am, one who shows respect to my teachers and my employers. This is a direct reflection on how a child was disciplined at home. Because my parents took the time to correct my siblings and myself, they did not have to receive a phone call from the Oakland County Police Department, calling my father to pick us up. I thank God for that. There may be times when we were growing up that we badly needed discipline in school, but this was totally out of the teacher's hands. My father came to the school and immediately took action and we behaved ourselves correctly, henceforth and forevermore.

I also remember that during elementary school, correcting a child was legal. If the student was out of line, the teachers took action upon themselves to use the paddle on us to get us back in line we we would act properly in the schools. Now, it's illegal because parents feel that discipline is abuse. But looking at the difference in society now and when I was in school, about 15 years ago, I can see how correcting children with spanking or paddling has surely been removed from the schools and probably the home, also.

I heartily applaud my parents on chastising me when I needed it the most. This is the final scripture from the bible that I will share with you, *Hebrews 12:6-11, For whom the Lord loveth he chasteneth, and scourgeth every son whom he receiveth. V7. If ye endure chastening, God dealeth with you as with sons; for what son is he whom the father chasteneth not? V8. But if ye be without chastisement, whereof all are partakers, then are ye bastards and not sons. V9. Furthermore, we have had fathers of our flesh which corrected us, and we gave them reverence: shall we not much rather be in subjection unto the Father of spirits, and live? V10. For they verily for a few days chastiseth us after their own pleasure; but he for our profit, that we might be partakers of his holiness. V11. Now no chastening for the present seemeth to be joyous, but grievous: nevertheless afterward it yieldeth the peaceable fruit of righteousness unto them which are exercised thereby.*

In conclusion, discipline is good. At the hour it is being applied, the child may hate the parents but in the long run, after they've raised their own children, they will take the time to thank their parents for the very performance that made them grieve as a child, for it was very much needed and it is now very much appreciated.

"A NOTE FROM A POET'S HEART"

Have you ever arrived in a strange territory with no one there to guide you or to even welcome you? Have you ever gone into a restaurant and kept looking at the door, hoping that someone would walk in and ask, "Is this seat taken?"

Have you ever looked at the stars and wished that you had someone there to confide in?

Have you ever gone on vacation and lay on the beach, watching the waves and wishing that you had someone special to share this relaxing experience with?

Well, I don't know about you but that special person that I've always pictured, or imagined, that friend that I needed, the one who would always be there for me even though at the time he wasn't - I just wanted to tell you that I feel that person is you!

When I first started working at the hospital, things were very strange to me; I really didn't have anyone to confide in. I didn't have anyone to share my thoughts or my jokes with, anyone who would actually laugh with me and be 'for real'. I never thought that I could actually have lunch with my coworkers without knowing that they weren't two-faced or jealous of me and not try to out do me but would work with me, no matter what came up.

I remember some evenings that you would ask me if I wanted to take a walk with you. I really was nervous the first time, but when we strolled down the halls of St. Joseph, I felt like when I was with you, I had come home. So much peace and even though I had no words to share with you, I knew that you enjoyed my company as much as I did yours. As you so graciously gave me tours of each floor, I would pray that time would stand still. I didn't want your shift to be over.

There were conversations that I remember when I could feel that you were truly pouring out your heart and that you needed someone to confide in, or you needed answers or perhaps, just someone to talk to. Well, I felt honored. I have never had a friendship as special as the one we have. I am not writing to cause you to be teary-eyed, but I know that the Lord has merged our paths so that our friendship may grow.

I've tried so hard to go away to attend the University of Missouri. I've planned it all for over a year now. Since my divorce, I have felt that I had to run away from everything. I got tired of people reminding me of the man I'd married, or the cause of the divorce, or "Couldn't you both at least have tried to work it out?"

Questions that no one would ever be able to answer because that is, indeed, in my past. Sometimes, I would bring it up during our conversations and it's not like I'm missing that part of my life at all, but to me, it's a testimony of how God has brought me through these trials and if I made it, so can you.

When I'm at home in my bedroom, I glance down at all of the college courses and at the campus and believe me, I have at least five colleges that I could have attended that cross my mind daily: Oakland Community College, Oakland University, Northwood University, Davenport University and Madonna University.

You would not believe the stress that comes with wanting to do something and being afraid I can't achieve it, or being afraid of failing. For many years, I've been hard on myself and I know now that this wasn't right.

It seemed that everything that I started I wouldn't finish. It was like I was scared of accomplishing it or afraid that I would let others and myself down if everything wasn't where it should be. Example: after graduating from Pontiac Northern High, June 1992, I didn't know exactly what to do with my life. I always felt that my parents wanted me to do exactly what my sister did, for some strange reason, (now I know that it was just my imagination).

I was enrolled at Oakland Technical Center, taking two courses. In the eleventh grade, I was taking a course in Nursing Assistant/Health Occupation.

Well, that was fine until my externship at Avondale Convalescent Home. As you know, I have a weak stomach. I couldn't take the odor or the duties that were involved in caring for the ill and the elderly. So I am a Certified Nursing Assistant.

Then, in the twelfth grade I enrolled in a two-year program in Cosmetology. My mother strongly urged me to do this. At first it was ok, but then it started to really bother me. After the first year, I dropped out. Two years later, I went back and finished the second year but I never got my license. I went to state boards and passed the written exam and almost passed the practical exam. You just don't know how it made me feel, knowing that my parents had accompanied me all the way up to the location of the exam, and also knowing that I hadn't accomplished a thing (or so I thought).

In September 1992, I was enrolled at Ross Medical Educational Center and took the course to become a Medical/Dental Administrative Assistant. This was such a great experience for me. For the first time in my life, I finished school with a 4.0 GPA. I nearly died; I didn't think such a thing was possible! Afterwards, it was time for me to make money and support myself. Mind you, my parents said that I didn't have to work if

I didn't want to. I was, indeed, what you would call a spoiled brat!

I worked at Comerica Bank for two years in the Collection Support Dept, filing HFA claims, credit life and disability claims, preparing liens and delinquent accounts, etc.

I've also worked at First Security Bank (my first job).

I've seen God's favor in my life. I worked as a temporary employee in their mailroom, and then I was promoted to Payment Processor etc. I stayed there for two years and then moved on to Comerica.

I worked at Chrysler Tech. as a summer temporary job while I was in school. That was, Indeed, the most beautiful building that I've ever seen. I worked at Quest Diagnostics Laboratory and this was a good job. I have worked as an insurance biller, first in Medicare/Medical Necessity department and then in the Blue Shield department. I was promoted to the Quality Control department and volunteered to work in the Patient Phones department. I stayed at that job for three years. I have learned so much!

Have you ever experienced being at a job and after a time, it feels that there's no point in you remaining there because there is no room for growth in the company. That is why I have switched to so many companies.

Finally I arrived at where I am now. When I started I worked three nights a week, part- time. I was preparing to go to Cancun during August, 2000 with my cousin and I needed some extra money. Just before that, I was working at Rite-Aid Pharmacy on Woodward as a Pharmacy Technician. However, I didn't like how my group leaders and managers were treating the patients concerning their prescriptions, so I left and began working full-time at St Joe. I left Quest because there was no room for growth, unless the employee had a four-year degree in Sales, then he or she could transfer.

Since I've been at St. Joe, I've had the opportunity to see how people act and react to different circumstances. I've seen people betrayed and lied to. I've seen them rewarded and I've seen those who abuse the system, (not calling any names). Ha Ha. You've volunteered your time and voice in sharing in my free time, here at work.

Well it wasn't really free time. It was time when we took a break or a breather.

You have informed me about things and you've always made me laugh, probably while not trying to, and I really appreciate that.

When I thought about going away to school, I thought that there I might meet someone who could be a friend to me and then I wouldn't have to worry about not having anyone to share things with. I started really getting stressed out by all of the sudden changes that I would have to make and I began to wonder how I would be able to manage, so far from home Then I thought to myself, if I were to live in St. Louis I'd never find anyone to replace (or take the place) of the friend that I've made at St. Joseph Hospital.

So will you stand up, look in the mirror and let me introduce you as the friend that has made a difference in my life; you have no idea know how much you have encouraged me to move forward. Just saying 'Thank you' is never enough; you'll always have a place in my heart. At first I was going to present this to one specific person but that would be very prejudiced. Especially when it just wasn't one person who has inspired me, encouraged me and made me feel loved, appreciated and needed, and been made to understand that you have enjoyed my company. So this is dedicated to everyone who's ever had a part of my life. I may have forgotten many of the names but never the prayers that went up on my behalf. My family, coworkers, friends and classmates at Northwood University. I love you all and I'll see ya'.

DEDICATION TO MY GRANDFATHER

From my earliest memories, you have been a person who took as much time as you needed to, to help those in need. You would fix their cars, even when you really didn't want to. You have a heart straight from God.

The long hours that I've sat watching television with you, talking with you for innumerable hours, listening to your words of wisdom. For the dinners that you've cooked to fill my stomach and the wisdom that has filled my mind, you'll never be forgotten.

For the many whippings that you had to give me, even when you said that it was hurting you more than me; I knew that you would always see the good in everything even when at the time, I didn't. The laughter and the peace that you've brought to my heart, knowing that whatever you encouraged me in, I would have for all time to come. You never put me down or made me feel bad. You've always told me that I was too good to put up with less, that I was worth being loved and held, not being treated me as a dog by anyone.

You always shared great memories of you and grandma. You've always shown much love to her and to your family. You've showed us how to live a holy life and attend church daily. You've shown me how to make gumbo and green fried tomatoes. These are treasures in my heart. I love to eat shrimp, broccoli and the ultimate, cheese and sausage dinners, or just snacks with you.

You are a family man, a good husband and a good grandfather and great grent-grandfather. You always took the time to baby-sit us, feed us or even spank us. There was never a time that I didn't want to go over to my grandparent's house. Besides knowing that there would always be food on the table, satellite television and laughter in the air, the greatest treasure was love.

Granddad, you gave me away at my wedding. I've never taken that gift for granted. Even though the marriage didn't work out, you never put me down or belittled me; instead, you encouraged me and wiped the tears that fell from my eyes. You told me how beautiful I am, and that I should give it some time and the right man will come my way and sweep me off my feet, and there will always be love for me in your house.

"Wait on God," you said, "he'll direct your steps."

You told me that you are proud of me and of all my achievements. You've always told me to keep my head up and to not look back. Well, the only thing that I look back on are the memories that will never leave my heart, of all the times that I spent with my grand-daddy.

I'll see you in heaven. I love you forever.

Thank you,

Love

Your granddaughter

MY FAVORITE SCRIPTURES FROM

THE BIBLE

The Lord recompense thy work, and a full reward be given thee of the Lord God of Israel, under whose wings thou art come to trust. Ruth 2:12

If my people, which are called by my name, shall humble themselves and pray, and seek my face, and turn from their wicked ways; then will I hear from heaven, and will forgive their sin and will heal their land. 2 Chronicles 7:14

And he said, Hearken ye, all Judah, and ye inhabitants of Jerusalem, and thou king Jehoshaphat, Thus saith the Lord unto you, Be not afraid nor dismayed by reason of this great multitude; for the battle is not yours, but God's. 2 Chronicles 20:15

Believe in the lord your God, so shall ye be established; believe his prophets, so shall ye prosper. 2 Chronicles 20:20b

In what place therefore ye hear the sound of the trumpet, resort ye thither unto us; our God shall fight for us. Nehemiah 4:20

For this day is holy unto our Lord: neither be ye sorry; for the joy of the Lord is your strength. Nehemiah 8:10b

For God speaketh once, yea twice, yet man perceiveth it not. In a dream, in a vision of the night, when deep sleep falleth upon men, in slumbering upon the bed; Then he openeth the ears of men, and sealeth their instruction, That he may withdraw man from his purpose, and hide pride from man. Job 33:14-17

For his eyes are upon the ways of man, and he seeth all his goings. Job 34:21

Blessed is the man that walketh not in the counsel of the ungodly, nor standeth in the of sinners, nor sitteth in the seat of the scornful. But his delight is in the law of the Lord; and in his law doth he meditate day and night. And he shall be like a tree planted by rivers of water, that bringeth forth his fruit in his season; whatsoever he doeth shall prosper. The ungodly are not so: but are like the chaff which the wind driveth away. Therefore the ungodly shall not stand in the judgment, or sinners in the congregation of the righteous. For the Lord knoweth the way of the righteous: but the way of the ungodly shall perish. Psalm 1:1-6

For thou, Lord, wilt bless the righteous; with favour wilt thou compass him as with a *shield.* Psalm 5:12

O Lord our Lord, how excellent is thy name in all the name! Who hast set thy glory above the heavens. Out of the mouth of babes and sucklings hast thou ordained

strength because of thine enemies, that thou mightest still the enemy and the avenger. When I consider thy heavens, the work of thy fingers, the moon and the stars, which thou hast ordained. What is man, that thou art mindful of him? For thou hast made him a little lower than the angels, and hast crowned him with glory and honour. Thou madest him to have domino over the works of thy hands; thou hast put all things under his feet; All sheep and oxen, yea, and the beasts of the field; The fowl of the air, and the fish of the sea, and whatsoever passeth through the paths of the seas. O Lord our Lord, how excellent is thy name in all the earth! Psalms 8:1-9*

Thou hast given him his heart's desire, and has not witholden the request of his lips. Psalms 21:2

Unto thee, O Lord, do I lift up my soul. O my God, I trust in thee: let me not be ashamed, let not mine enemies triumph over me. Yea, let none that wait on thee be ashamed: let them be ashamed which transgress without cause. Shew me thy ways, O Lord; teach me thy paths. Lead me in thy truth, and teach me: for thou art the God of my salvation; on thee do I wait all the day. Remember, O Lord, thy tender mercies and thy loving kindnesses; for thy have been ever of old. Psalms 25:1-6

The Lord is my light and my salvation; whom shall I fear? The Lord is the strength of my life; of whom shall I be afraid? When the wicked, even mine enemies and my foes, came upon me to eat up my flesh, they stumbled and fell. Though an host should encamp against me, my heart shall not fear: though war should rise against me, in this will I be confident. One thing have I desired of the Lord, that will I seek after; that I may dwell in the house of the

Sandra LaFaye Crump

Lord all the days of my life, to behold the beauty of the Lord, and to enquire in his temple. For in the time of trouble he shall hide me in his pavilion: in the secret of his tabernacle shall he hide me; he shall set me up upon a rock. And now shall mine head be lifted up above mine enemies round about me; therefore will I offer in his tabernacle sacrifices of joy; I will sing, yea, I will sing praises unto the Lord. Psalms27:1-6

Teach me thy way, O Lord, and lead me in a plain path, because of mine enemies. Deliver me not over unto the will of mine enemies: for false witnesses are risen up against me, and such as breathe out cruelty. I had fainted, unless I had believed to see the goodness of the Lord in the land of the living. Wait on the Lord: be of good courage, and he shall strengthen thine heart: wait, I say, on the Lord. Psalms 27:11-14

Many are the afflictions of the righteous: but the Lord delivereth him out of them all. Psalms 34:19

Fret not thyself because of evildoers, neither be thou envious against the workers of iniquity. For they shall soon be cut down like the grass, and wither as the green herb. Trust in the Lord, and do good; so shall thou dwell in the land, and verily thou shall be *fed. Delight thyself also in the Lord; and he shall give thee the desires of thine heart. Commit thy way unto the Lord; trust also in him; and he shall bring it to pass.* Psalms 37:1-5

My soul thirsteth for God, for the living God: when shall I come and appear before God? Psalms 42:2

*Blessed the Lord, O my soul: and all that is within me, bless his holy name. Bless the Lord, O my soul, and forget not all his benefits: Who forgiveth all thine iniquities; who healeth all thy diseases; Who redeemeth thy life from destruction; who **crowneth** the with loving kindness and tender mercies; Who satisfieth thy mouth with good things; so that thy youth is renewed like the eagle's. The Lord executeth righteousness and judgment for all that are oppressed. Psalms 103:1-6*

Who can find a virtuous woman? For her price is far above rubies. Favour is deceitful, and beauty is vain: but a woman that feareth the Lord, she shall be praised. Proverbs 31:10,30

If ye be willing and obedient, ye shall eat the good of the land. Isaiah 1:19

Behold, God is my salvation; I will trust, and not be afraid: for the Lord Jehovah is my strength and my song; he also is become my salvation. Therefore with joy shall ye draw water out of the wells of salvation. Isaiah 12:2,3

And it shall come to pass in that day, that his burden shall be taken away from off thy shoulder, and his yoke from off thy shoulder, and his yoke from off thy neck, and the yoke shall be destroyed because of the anointing. Isaiah 10:27

Fear thou not; for I am with thee: be not dismayed; for I am thy God: I will strengthen thee; yea, I will help thee; year, I will uphold thee with the right hand of my righteousness. Isaiah 41:10

No weapon that is formed against thee shall prosper: and every tongue that shall rise against thee in judgment thou shalt condemn. This is the heritage of the servants of the Lord, and their righteousness is of me, saith the Lord. Isaiah 54:17

Arise, shine; for thy light is come, and the glory of the Lord is risen upon thee. Isaiah 60:1.

The Spirit of the lord God is upon me; because the Lord hath anointed me to preach good tidings unto the meek; he hath sent me to bind up the brokenhearted, to proclaim liberty to the captives, and the opening of the prison to them that are bound. To proclaim the acceptable year of the Lord, and the day of vengeance of our God: to comfort all that mourn; To appoint unto them that mourn in Zion, to give unto them beauty for ashes, the oil of joy for mourning, the garment of praise for the spirit of heaviness; that they might be called tress of righteousness, the planting of the Lord, that he might be glorified. Isaiah 61:1-3

Before I formed thee in the belly I knew thee; and before thou camest forth out of the womb I sanctified thee, and I ordained thee a prophet unto the nations. Jeremiah 1:5

And I will give you pastors according to mine heart, which shall feed you with knowledge and understanding. Jeremiah 3:15

Call unto me, and I will answer thee, and shew thee great and mighty things, which thou knowest not. Jeremiah 33:3

It is of the Lord's mercies that we are not consumed, because his compassions fail not. They are new every morning: great is thy faithfulness. The Lord is my portion, saith my soul; therefore will I hope in him. The Lord is good unto them that wait for him, to the soul that seeketh him. Lamentations 3:22-25

Jesus said unto him, If thou canst believe, all things are possible to him that believeth. Mark 9:23

And Jesus looking upon them saith, With men it is impossible, but not with God: for with God all things are possible. Mark 10:27

And Jesus answering saith unto them, Have faith in God. For verily I say unto you, That whosoever shall say unto this mountain, Be thou removed, and be thou cast into the sea; and shall not doubt in his heart, but shall believe that those things which he saith shall come to pass; he shall have whatsoever he saith. Therefore I say unto you what things soever ye desire, when ye pray, believe that ye receive them, and ye shall have them.

And when ye stand praying, forgive, if ye have ought against any: that your Father also which is in heaven may forgive you your trespasses. But if ye do not forgive, neither will your Father which is in heaven forgive your trespasses. Mark 11:22-226

And the angel came in unto her, and said, Hail, thou that art highly favored, the Lord is with thee: blessed art thou among women. And when she saw him, she was troubled at his saying, and cast in her mind what manner of salutation this should be. And the angel said unto her, Fear not, Mary: for thou hast found favour with God. And, behold, thou shalt conceive in thy womb, and bring forth a son, and shall call his name Jesus. He shall be great, and shall be called the Son of the Highest; and the Lord God shall give unto the throne of his father David: And he shall reign over the house of Jacob for ever; and of his kingdom there shall be no end. Then said Mary unto the angel, How shall this be, seeing I know not a man? And the angel answered and said unto her, The Holy Ghost shall come upon thee. And the power of the highest shall overshadow thee: therefore also that holy thing which shall be born of thee shall be called the Son of God. And, behold, thy cousin Elisabeth, she hath also conceived a son in her old age: and this is the sixth month with her, who was called barren. For with God nothing shall be impossible. Luke 1:28-37

And Simon answering said unto him, Master, we have toiled all the nigh, and have taken nothing: nevertheless at thy word I will let down the net. Luke 5:5

For God so loved the world, that he gave his only begotten Son, that whosever believeth in him should not perish, but have everlasting life. John 3:16

There is therefore now no condemnation to them which are in Christ Jesus, who walk not after the flesh, but after the Spirit. Romans 8:1

For we are saved by hope: but hope that is seen is not hope: for what a man seeth, why doth he yet hope for? But if we hope for that we see not, then do we with patience wait for it. Like wise the Spirit also helpeth our infirmities: for we know not what we should pray for as we ought: but the Spirit itself maketh intercession for us with groanings which cannot be uttered. And he that searcheth the hearts knoweth what is the mind of the Spirit, because he maketh intercession for the saints according to the will of God. And we know that all things work together for good to them that love God, to them who are the called according to his purpose. Romans 8:24-28

Therefore, my beloved brethren, be ye steadfast, unmovable, always abounding in the work of the lord, forasmuch as ye know that your labour is not in vain in the Lord. 1 Corinthians 15:58

For all the promises of God in him are yea, and in him Amen, unto the glory of God by us. 2 Corinthians 1:20

Therefore if any man be in Christ, he is a new creature: old things are passed away; behold, all things are become new. And all things are of God, who hath reconciled us to himself by Jesus Christ, and hath given to us the ministry of reconciliation. 2 Corinthians 5:17,18

For though we walk in the flesh, we do not war after the flesh: (For the weapons of our warfare are not carnal, but mighty through God to the pilling down of strong holds;) Casting down imaginations, and every high thing that exalteth itself against the knowledge of God, and bringing into captivity every thought to the obedience of Christ; And having in a readiness to revenge all disobedience, when your obedience is fulfilled. 2 Corinthians 10:3-6.

117

And he said unto me, My grace is sufficient for thee: for my strength is made perfect in weakness. 2 Corinthians 12:9a. For by grace are ye saved through faith; and that not of yourselves: it is the gift of God. Ephesians 2:8

That he would grant you, according to the riches of his glory, to be strengthened with might by his Spirit in the inner man: That Christ may dwell in your hearts by faith; that ye, being rooted and grounded in love, May be able to comprehend with all saints what is the breadth, and length, and depth, and height; And to know the love of Christ, which passeth knowledge, that ye might be filled with all the fullness of God. Now unto him that is able to do exceeding abundantly above all that we ask or think, according to the power that worketh in us. Ephesians 3:17-20

Be careful for nothing; but in every thing by prayer and supplication with thanksgiving let your requests be made known unto God. And the peace of God, which passeth all understanding, shall keep your hearts and minds thorough Christ Jesus. Philippians 4:6,7

I can do all things through Christ which strengthenth me. Philippians 4:13

But my God shall supply all your need according to his riches in glory by Christ Jesus. Philippians 4:19

Favorite tapes of the ministry that have

blessed my soul

These are the favorite tapes of the ministry that I can remember by title, that have made a difference in my life. All is hot, this is only to name a few. These have really made an impact on my life.

1. *Who can find a virtuous woman?"

2. "Forgetting those things which are behind"

3. "Examine yourselves"

4. "Open heart surgery"

5. "God sets the member in the body"

6. "Expect Turnaround"

7. "After the Test is Passed"

8. "Your change has come"

I hope that you enjoyed this book and my testimony.

May God continue to bless and increase you more and more, you and your children. Psalms 115:14

One word that I leave with you that was ministered to me and my church family that I shall always remember...**stand up and believe in your heart and confess that I ...**

"Expect

Turnaround"

Thank you,

Yours truly,

Sandra LaFaye Crump, 2002

WHAT LOVE MEANS TO ME?

By Sandra Crump

January 2002

(Now I know why I couldn't publish my book, I didn't put this in it)

Thank you Lord

What does LOVE mean to me? Well, this is, indeed, a very difficult word to give only Definition. When I was in the beauty salon getting my hair done, the subject of LOVE came up and those who had experienced it responded with their stories. Some didn't want to admit it becausee, yes indeed, this is a very touchy subject.

There are some who've experienced it and it's wounded them for life. What I mean is, no matter what goes on in life, there are always opportunity for this wonderful experience.

There are some who enter into other relationships while they are still are in love with another person. Is this right? Can this be justified? This is Love. I really don't have the answer to such an act. This word is so powerful that it would or could have you put a hindrance on your future.

I've entered into relationships with young men and they would say that they loved me, but who knows? The ones who hurt you are the ones who don't understand why, but they claim that they love you.

Love causes you to do things that you regret, or things that others think are just plain ignorant. I've been in relationships and others have asked me, why? You could have done better, they say, but when someone has your heart and this is all that you can think about, and things don't go the way they should, you're torn and doomed for life.

What I mean is that no matter who the next person is that you enter into a relationship with, you'll still be afraid to fully commit and when you finally do commit, you'll never know why - you may even be thinking of another.

While growing up, I watched my parents. This Love thing is very important and it shouldn't be taken lightly. There were many ups and downs throughout my parent's marriage, but I really admired them. No matter who was right or wrong, Love kept them together. Love brought me into the world.

Love isn't just a word used to describe intimacy between two persons. Love is a feeling that is shared.

It may be shared mutually or it may be one-sided. It is something that people tend to misuse and abuse.

During the time I was married, I experienced real love. I was always the type of person who took things to heart. I was very sentimental. There are a lot of things that people take for granted, such as: calling before going to bed to say I Love You. Asking how my day went? Revealing who the real ME is and knowing that what answers I've received were always honest and not just plain criticism.

Love causes you to accept things that shouldn't happen. Love causes you to be blind to everything that is all around you; love has you ignore things that are hurting you but because of Love, you will compromise. Love causes you to love unconditionally.

From my marriage and divorce, I've realized that I've loved unconditionally.

Regardless of what was said to me, no matter what offended me, because I Loved I was blind to it.

Even though Love is there, it must be mutual, especially in a marriage; otherwise, it is in vain.

This letter isn't just focusing on my marriage, but on myself. Self-examination is something that is truly needed in a person's life, especially when Love is present.

Sometimes it will cause you put all of your hopes and dreams on hold, so that Love can remain and the relationship will not take a wrong turn.

Even after my marriage had ended and I had gone to God and asked him to forgive me, even though I felt that I had given my all and had tried to make the marriage last, I still had feelings of regret. I thought that perhaps I should have dated someone else, and maybe I would have not have accepted the person that I married and life would have been different.

Hey, even though there are choices that we make, God honors these choices. He gives us choices; if not, he wouldn't be just. He's a just and faithful God so He gives us choices to make. Just as he gives us choices to make him our Lord and Savior in our life, or we can choose to take the other route - the one that isn't planned for us - just to please ourselves, and then we end up in hell with this on our conscience. Man, I made the choice of doing my own thing and being the Woman who I wanted to be, just so I could have all that I wanted out of life, without submission, without obedience, without a Pastor, without honesty, without Christ.

Yes, that is right. Jesus Christ took time to live his throne on high, to be a ransom for man. He gave his life for us so that we may have his life; why would one choose the other? Why? He showed us Love, He is Love.

Whenever I travel to Jamaica, Cancun, the Bahamas or wherever, I've noticed that there are men who say, Hey I love you, I want to marry you. Do they even know what they are saying? What if I was hard up for a man, like I've always heard that some women would take anyone just to say they have someone. Anyway, where would I be?

Would I be living in God's purpose? Would I be in line or in the place that God has for me? I don't think so.

Things run smoothly when you're in the place where God has put you. All of your needs are met. Blessings run you over continually. True Love is present. Don't get me wrong, even if you're in the place that God has for you, if you still enter into a relationship that isn't from God, things won't work for you. Usually, if YOU try to do it, then it won't work but if God is in control, it will all be good.

I am approached often and it's flattering, but he was not the one who's destined to fulfill purpose in my life. I wonder a lot, thinking, what am I supposed to be doing or who am I supposed to be in life? I think, am I doing what I was put here on earth to do?

These questions seem to be harder for me to answer than Love. But what I do think is, once I hook up, as I say, and meet the Man who is truly my destiny, then things will start falling into place. All my questions will be answered, and all of my OOO's will become WOW's.

Yes, I am terrified of going back down that road called meeting the person who I am to be in Love with, and truly Love forever but God knows and this causes me to have peace, so I just go on being faithful in the ministry, staying in the Word of God and in the Will of God. I know that I will be approached even more but when I meet that person, there will be PEACE and then the LOVE will flow and the JOY of being a wife will return.

Sometimes I get flashbacks and then I wonder, What IF? But God knows how to handle me in that situation; he covers it with the Blood. He causes me to forget all of the hurt and shame and embarrassment and the loneliness and the depression and the sickness that came out of all the Love that I've experienced in the past. Then he puts me in the present and shows me in the Word and in the preaching and teachings that comes from my Pastor, the good things that God has for me and how it is WORTH THE WAIT. Knowing that my better days are coming my way. How I am to FORGET THOSE THINGS THAT ARE BEHIND? How GOD MULTIPLIES MY SEED SOWN. How He'll give me DOUBLE FOR MY TROUBLE and how I am to EXPECT TURNAROUND.

So day by day, this LOVE thing keeps coming upon me I don't worry because when it's time, it's time and it's my season, it's just time for me to continue preparing myself and staying at the Brazen Laver (PC smile, I'm learning and listening) where I can find out WHO I am and Who God wants me to be.

So Love…what is it, exactly? This is, indeed, the hardest word to define. But what I learned from it is that What Jesus did for me is Love. What my parents have done in my life is Love. What my sisters and brothers and brothers-in-law have done for me is love.

That my niece and nephews have been in my life is Love. It's not just falling in love, but showing people love and being there for them. It may not always mean being there for them in person, but also in prayer.

There were a lot of people who I've called friend and they've made a huge impact in my life. And after growing up and maturing, I look back on why some of those friendships went downwards. Then I think back on that awesome, revealing dream I had, which occurred to me more than once.

The dream goes as follows. I was at home with my family, of course, living a life that is of God. Serving God in my youth, being everyone's friend. Letting everyone's problems dwell upon me. I didn't know how to handle the pressures of being a friend. I would let people walk over me, talk down to me, make fun of me, criticize me very wrongly and then hang out with them later.

After I would go home and head up to my bedroom, I would hold on to the handrails, which will be referred to as the banister. No problem, right? WRONG! As I hold on to the railing I would walk a little, then fall down, get up and fall again. I would just sit there at the bottom wondering, What is the problem? I know that I can climb these stairs, but it would work better if I hold on to the banister. So what is wrong here? Then I would just go back and try it later and the same thing would happen over again. Then I would wake up. I would go to sleep the following nights and have the same dream with the same ending, then finally I would make it about halfway up and the banister would break in half and I would fall. So I prayed and asked God to help me out. This dream is very weird. I know that I know how to go to my room, but I can't make it up those steps.

So he began to show me that I had to analyze exactly what was going on, piece by piece.

So here it is.

- I am an average, single Christian woman.
- I am doing what God wants me to do as a saved, Christian woman.
- I go about my life living holy and honest.
- But one thing that I lack. I am always trying to walk through life by holding on to the banister.

- What is the Bannister? Bannister is the people whom I depend upon.
- The stairs are my way of life, the things that I must go through and live by.
- Each step represent things that may be trials or triumphs.
- The door to my bedroom is the place where God wants me to go and it's the person whom I need to be, in the end. It's the victories that I'll share. It's the prosperity. It's the testimonies that I can witness to, for others to come through at a later day. It's the final me. It's the perfected me. It's who Christ intended for me to be.

So what was the problem. My problem wasn't with people. The long nights that I cried out to the Lord, wondering why a person had offended me? Why are they too hard headed and full of pride to admit to it, and why didn't they quit treating me that way.

Why am I the only one offended? Why should I always be the bigger one, and apologize.

THEN IT HIT ME!!!! I was walking my daily journey in life and each new day I would come and start to climb. No problem. I would put one foot first, No problem. I would hold on to the Bannister. Problem!!! I would use people to be my Bannister. I would hold on to them and wouldn't go on, till I had their blessing or their permission. I would need them to let me know that they approved, or that they will be there for me, in order for me to do this or that. Well, this is a problem. This was why it wasn't working for me. I would hold on to people and not to the Lord. Then each step, each trial I would need those people to be there, otherwise I couldn't go on. I could never reach the place where I needed to be because I would have people ahead of me. Then I wondered, so why is it that I would make it halfway and then the banister would break in half and I would fall. Well, this was the easy part, when holding on to people I was given false hope, hope that everything would be alright and then later, pride would set in and the banister would break. It was God bringing me down.

Anytime someone who would make it in life and then allow pride to step in, he's been exalted by himself. And Self cannot please God, or I should say, Flesh can't please God, only Faith. So God would bring me down, to humble me, to see what is in my heart, so I would examine myself and get it right. Put him first, *"Seek first the Kingdom and his righteousness and all these things will be added to me." Matthew 6:33.*

So I was instructed by God was to allow him to fix my mess. I was the modern day Humpty Dumpty. I relied upon all the king horses and the kings' men to fix my life and to be there for me, instead of allowing the King "Jesus" to be the one to do it and to be my head, and more than that, my Life. He's number one in my life.

So I allowed God to remake my banister. He is the Banister and I started holding on to Jesus. Each day, I would start my life off with him, PRIORITY. So as I take each day, I won't be afraid because the steps aren't just trials, but triumphs. It's words that people say, "Oh she's acting funny; she acts like she can't be here with us anymore."

It wasn't that. I'll be there but I'm not depending on you to make or break me.

You're not the one who's dominating my life, but the Lord. He is Lord. So I would take the words that "Oh, she'll never make it. She'll never be anything because of this or that."

I use all of that nonsense as stepping stones. I also use *Isaiah 54:17 "No weapon, that is formed against me shall prosper. And every tongue that rises up against me, in judgment I shall condemn."* (I really love this scripture, my mother gave me a t-shirt that had this scripture on it and she told me whenever I feel that the words of people, or of the enemy begins to get me down, put this shirt on and confess Isaiah 54:17. *Condemn those words. Put the Blood of Jesus on it*...Mom, I love you for that and for so much more)...

So I went to sleep and the dream finally had a happy ending. I went up the stairs and instead of holding on to people, I started holding on Jesus and to the Word of God. I took each step, which the devil meant as a stumbling block, but I used it as a stepping stone to overcome him by saying IT IS WRITTEN…and confessing the Word of God over my life and my situation, instead of coming to man with it and asking for advice, which sometimes was wrongful advice, which set me back at that time but now, I am able to come out ahead. I am more than a conqueror. I am victorious. I am mighty and great, only in the Lord and MY STEPS ARE ORDERED BY GOD. So what if I am still single, I have the Joy of the Lord. I know who I am. And when it's time for me to become a married woman, I'll know how to fight the enemy who may try to attack, (and he WILL try), but I have a *Isaiah 54:17* to counterattack, because I've used this Word many times while being single. So as Reverend Nelson always tells me, to encourage me, how I've witnessed that word being manifested in his life, with his new WOW…It is indeed WORTH THE WAIT and this is why I call this book, HAPPILY EVER AFTER…Because no matter what I've been through or have to go through in the future, I'll be happy because I know the end result. I've read the end of the book…

WE WIN!!!!!!!!!!!!!!!!!!!!!!!

Thank you for reading and I hope that you've learned something and gotten something

out of this book. It's not that LOVE is hard to define. When you know Love (Jesus as Lord and

Savior), the other Love will flow smoothly….